Debating the Ku Klux Klan

Also from Westphalia Press
westphaliapress.org

The Idea of the Digital University

Masonic Tombstones and Masonic Secrets

Eight Decades in Syria

Avant-Garde Politician

L'Enfant and the Freemasons

Baronial Bedrooms

Conflicts in Health Policy

Material History and Ritual Objects

Paddle Your Own Canoe

Opportunity and Horatio Alger

Careers in the Face of Challenge

Bookplates of the Kings

Collecting American Presidential Autographs

Misunderstood Children

Original Cables from the Pearl Harbor Attack

Social Satire and the Modern Novel

The Amenities of Book Collecting

The Genius of Freemasonry

A Definitive Commentary on Bookplates

James Martineau and Rebuilding Theology

No Bird Lacks Feathers

Earthworms, Horses, and Living Things

The Man Who Killed President Garfield

Anti-Masonry and the Murder of Morgan

Understanding Art

Homeopathy

Ancient Masonic Mysteries

Collecting Old Books

The Boy Chums Cruising in Florida Waters

The Thomas Starr King Dispute

Ivanhoe Masonic Quartettes

Lariats and Lassos

Mr. Garfield of Ohio

The Wisdom of Thomas Starr King

The French Foreign Legion

War in Syria

Naturism Comes to the United States

New Sources on Women and Freemasonry

Designing, Adapting, Strategizing in Online Education

Gunboat and Gun-runner

Meeting Minutes of Naval Lodge No. 4 F.A.A.M

Debating the
Ku Klux Klan

by Julia E. Johnsen

WESTPHALIA PRESS
An imprint of Policy Studies Organization

Debating the Ku Klux Klan
All Rights Reserved © 2014 by Policy Studies Organization

Westphalia Press
An imprint of Policy Studies Organization
1527 New Hampshire Ave., NW
Washington, D.C. 20036
info@ipsonet.org

ISBN-13: 978-1-63391-137-6
ISBN-10: 1633911373

Cover design by Taillefer Long at Illuminated Stories:
www.illuminatedstories.com

Daniel Gutierrez-Sandoval, Executive Director
PSO and Westphalia Press

Rahima Schwenkbeck, Director of Media and Marketing
PSO and Westphalia Press

Updated material and comments on this edition
can be found at the Westphalia Press website:
www.westphaliapress.org

KU KLUX KLAN
JULIA E. JOHNSEN, Compiler

INTRODUCTION

The Ku Klux Klan is an anomaly in American life. The extreme secrecy with which it is shrouded and the apparent spread of membership into the thousands in practically every state of the Union, with attempted entrance also into Canada and England, make it both difficult and important to bring into the open reliable facts and a clear comprehension of the inner nature of this extraneous social organism.

The present Ku Klux Klan embraces the organization founded in 1915 at Atlanta, Georgia, by Colonel William Joseph Simmons, professing to commemorate the historic Ku Klux Klan of reconstruction days. According to Colonel Simmons before the Rules Committee in Congress, its membership in 1921 was approximately ninety to ninety-five thousand. Its growth is augmented by a highly organized system of propaganda. Save for a few of the executive and organizing officials, its members are generally unknown. Among its late manifestations is the formation of an auxiliary woman's division known as the "Kamelia," and a movement styled the "Great American Fraternity" has also been ascribed to its activities.

The material on the Ku Klux Klan is frankly one-sided. The press is, as a rule, hostile or at best neutral. For its defense one must go to such publications and statements as emanate from within its own organism. A few organizations are actively combatting it. Foremost among these are the American Unity League, with offices at 127 North Dearborn Street, Chicago, which league also publishes a weekly paper "Tolerance," and the American Civil Liberties Union, 100 Fifth Avenue, New York. The Catholic, negro, and Jewish organizations also oppose it.

The present pamphlet has been included in the Reference Shelf in response to a demand for reference material on this subject. The attempt has been made by the compiler to avoid bias and let the facts speak for themselves to the discriminating, as is in keeping with the established practice of the debaters' series of publications. To this end representative material is included setting forth both the aims and defense of the Klan and the arguments of the opposition.

JULIA E. JOHNSEN

April 2, 1923

NOTE TO SECOND EDITION

The second edition has been enlarged by the inclusion of nineteen references and one reprint of more recent date.

JULIA E. JOHNSEN

May, 1924

BRIEF

RESOLVED: *That the Ku Klux Klan should be condemned by all right-thinking Americans.*

AFFIRMATIVE

I. The Ku Klux Klan should be condemned because its principles are destructive and wrong.
   A. It is founded on the principle of *invisible* government.
      1. Its membership is masked and unknown.
      2. It tries to control outside affairs.
         a. Legitimate secret societies do not arrogate to themselves control over external affairs.
      3. Membership is concealed under oath.
   B. It places itself above law.
      1. The Klan itself commits crime in the name of righteousness.
         a. Murder, kidnapping, violence, flogging, etc.
         b. It disregards lawfully elected officers and legal machinery.
      2. Klan loyalty is made more binding than civic loyalty.
         a. Members will not testify against one another.
      3. It is an arbitrary tribunal.
   C. It is irresponsible.
      1. There is no effective control of locals.
         a. Recalcitrant "dens" can only have their charters revoked.

(1) This is done only under pressure of public opinion.
(2) It does not prevent the members continuing activities, using regalia, etc.
2. In case of crime there is no punishment of offenders.
a. The Klan does not bring members to justice.
(1) Even when charged to pseudo members, no justice is meted out.
b. The community cannot locate the responsibility for crime.
D. It ignores fundamental rights of others.
1. Constitutional rights.
a. The right to protection by law.
b. To trial by jury.
c. To religious freedom.
2. The inherent personal right of every human being to liberty of thought, conscience and action, providing the rights of others are not interfered with.
3. The Klan is used for personal hatreds and prejudices.

II. Its activities are a menace.
A. It is disruptive.
1. It spreads religious prejudice.
a. By excluding non-protestant religions from membership.
b. By active propaganda against them of bigotry, intolerance, persecution.
2. It intensifies class feeling.
a. It discriminates against all persons of foreign birth and negroes.
3. It plays upon the particular prejudices of each locality.

4. It gives rise to community insecurity and suspicion.
    a. Men cannot trust even their neighbors.
B. It is a political menace.
  1. It undermines democratic government.
      a. Interferes in primaries, elections, intimidates voters, etc.
      b. Is a menace to political parties.
C. It dictates in other American institutions.
  1. In education.
      a. It is attempting to stamp out private schools in Oregon.
      b. It has dictated in regard to teaching forces and curricula.
D. There are no evils sufficient to justify its self-appointed work.
  1. Legal machinery has not failed.
  2. There is no Catholic, Jewish, negro, or foreign menace.
      a. Such claims are based upon ignorance or misrepresentation, or are disseminated for personal ends.
          (1) To gain adherents among those prejudiced against them.
          (2) To force them to "keep their place."
          (3) To cover the Klan's real plans.
  3. It is the honorable way to deal with corruption, etc., in the open, not by underground methods.

III. It is undesirable in every way.
A. It belies many of the ideals it pretends to uphold.
  1. Brotherhood is limited to membership.
  2. Americanism is of its own brand.

3. It breaks up homes by driving its victims to disgrace and banishment.
B. It fosters cowardice.
1. It leads men to condone its evils for fear of arousing its enmity.
2. It cannot live in the open.
a. Public opinion largely condemns it.
b. When membership is exposed members are forced to resign.
3. It is cowardly in punishment and acts.
C. The real reason for its existence is commercialism.
1. Heavy membership and degree fees and annual dues enrich its promoters.
2. The sale of regalia nets large profit.
D. The insidious power it acquires is a grave future danger.
1. It is susceptible to abuse at any time under wrong leadership.
a. Members must obey dictates or leave.
2. Its avowed ideals are no guarantee of observance.
a. It is well known that movements of high purpose degenerate with time.
(1) The Camorra is an example of such degeneration.
3. Its acquirement of power on a large scale would be a menace to government.

Negative

I. The Ku Klux Klan stands for exalted ideals.
A. It is an organization of the highest type.
1. It is on the same plan as other secret societies.
2. It commemorates the sacrifice, service and achievements of the original Klan.
3. It is legal.

KU KLUX KLAN

        a. Incorporated under the laws of Georgia.
    4. Its membership is of the highest type.
        a. Men of moral and social standing.
        b. In many cases officials of the nation, state, county and city.
    5. It has an exalted ritualistic form of work.
B. It is a practical fraternity. It tends:
    1. To promote the principles of brotherhood among its members.
    2. To protect womanhood and the home.
    3. To help the weak, suffering, and needy.
    4. To build a better citizenship.
        a. Inculcates respect for law.
        b. Encourages use of the ballot.
    5. To act as a vigilance committee.
    6. It is given to the practice of benevolence.
C. It upholds other high ideals.
    1. Patriotism.
        a. Allegiance to American institutions.
            (1) It aims to conserve, protect, and maintain the distinctive institutions and ideals of a pure Americanism.
        b. It is pledged to protect the Constitution and the flag.
        c. It stands for America first among nations.
    2. Christian ideals.
        a. While conceding the right of every man to worship in his own way, it upholds the Christian religion as opposed to Roman Catholicism.
        b. It encourages the study of the Bible.
    3. Racial ideals.
        a. The supremacy of the white race and of native-born Americans.

II. The activities and attitude of the Ku Klux Klan are justified.
   A. By the Catholic menace.
      1. The Klan is opposed to the domination in American life of a foreign ecclesiastical potentate.
      2. It opposes it with respect to the principle of the separation of church and state.
      3. It opposes the activities of the Jesuits, the most cunning, persistent and deceitful foes of Protestant Christianity.
      4. It opposes undue influence by the Knights of Columbus.
   B. By the negro problem.
      1. The Klan opposes negro majorities at the polls.
         a. The white race is the ruling race by inheritance.
         b. It can't be expected to surrender to another control of its vital and fundamental governmental affairs.
      2. It opposes the teaching of social equality.
         a. Certain negro organizations and periodicals attempt to sow seed of discontent and racial hatred by such teaching.
      3. The Klan is otherwise the friend of the negro.
         a. No law-abiding person of any race, creed or color has aught to fear from it.
   C. In relation to Jews.
      1. They are unproductive and money-getting.
      2. They do not subscribe to the Christian religion.
   D. In relation to the foreign element.

1. The Klan upholds 100 per cent Americanism.
    a. It is opposed to foreign idealism or allegiance.
    b. It advocates sensible and patriotic immigration laws.
  E. In relation to corruption and crime.
    1. There is much political corruption.
      a. Sometimes there is no redress for citizens but the Klan.
    2. There is government within government dictation, practically minority rule.
    3. Private immorality goes unpunished.
    4. Bootlegging is carried on.
III. In other ways the Klan is desirable.
  A. It is law-abiding.
    1. Lawless deeds have not and will not be committed by it.
      a. Mobs have not been ordered and directed by the Klan as an organization.
        (1) Many mobs have been put over by forces opposed to the Klan to discredit it.
        (2) They have been put over by indignant citizens to correct wrong.
        (3) They have been committed by lawless groups wrongfully appropriating its name.
    2. It is not designed to act in the capacity of a law-enforcement or moral correction agency except so far as members may assist regular officers of law to apprehend criminals and uphold law.
    3. The Rules Committee of Congress investigating it failed to file a report against it.

4. It has invited investigation by the Department of Justice and the Postoffice Department of its books, records, and files.
B. It has been misrepresented.
 1. Newspapers have never given their readers the truth about it.
 2. Its accusers are those who, through guilty conscience, fear it.
C. Its secrecy is not to be condemned.
 1. Its power lies in the secrecy with which it is surrounded.
  a. It is necessary to fight its enemies with their own weapons.
 2. The Knights of Columbus have an oath as binding as the Klan, if not more so.
D. There is no commercialism.
 1. The funds are properly and honorably handled in a business-like way.
 2. The dues collected are necessary in organization work.
 3. No official is profiting

BIBLIOGRAPHY

BIBLIOGRAPHIES

United States. Library of Congress. List of references on Knights of the Ku Klux Klan, exclusive of the original Ku Klux Klan, but including night riders, etc. 6p. typewritten. 70c. Public Affairs Information Service. New York. Feb. 16, 1923.

United States. Library of Congress. Select list of references on Ku Klux Klan. 8p. typewritten. 90c. Public Affairs Information Service. New York. June 20, 1913.

GENERAL REFERENCES

BOOKS AND PAMPHLETS

Beard, James Melville. K.K.K. sketches. 192p. Claxton, Remsen & Haffelfinger, Philadelphia. 1877.

Brawley, Benjamin. Ku Klux Klan. *In* Social history of the American negro. p. 272-8. Macmillan, New York. 1921.

Brown, William Garrott. Ku Klux movement. *In* Lower south in American history. p. 191-225. Macmillan, New York. 1902.

Brunson, R. J. Historic Pulaski: birthplace of the Ku Klux Klan. 108p. Methodist Pub. Nashville, Tenn. 1913.

Dixon, Thomas. Clansman: an historical romance of the Ku Klux Klan. 374p. Doubleday. 1916.

Fleming, Walter L. Revised and amended prescript of Ku Klux Klan. 31p. Morgantown, W.Va. Feb., 1904.

Howe, Elizabeth M. Ku Klux uniform. Buffalo Historical Society. Publications. 25:9-41. '21.

Lester, J. C. and Wilson, D. L. Ku Klux Klan: its origin, growth and disbandment. Introduction and notes by Walter L. Fleming. 198p. Neale, New York. 1905.

Mississippi Historical Society. Publications. 9: 109-71. '06. Enforcement act of 1871 and the Ku Klux Klan in Mississippi. J. S. McNeilly.

United States. Circuit Court. Ku Klux trials at Columbia, S.C. Official report. 224p. Columbia Union, Columbia, S.C. 1872.

United States. House of Representatives. Committee on rules. 67th Congress, 1st session. Hearings. Ku Klux Klan. 184p. Supt. of doc. 1921.

Periodicals

American Federationist. 29: 905-6. D. '22. Confirmation from a strange source.
<small>Protest against Gov. Allen's action in Kansas.</small>

Atlantic Monthly. 87: 634-44. My. '01. Ku Klux movement. William Garrott Brown.

Century Magazine. n.s. 6: 398-410. Jl. '84. Ku Klux Klan: its origin, growth, and disbandment. D. L. Wilson.

Chautauquan. 65: 170. Ja. '12. Ku Klux: poem. Madison Cawein.

Congressional Record. 63: 32-7. N. 22, '22. Situation in Louisiana.

Current History Magazine, New York Times. 14: 19-25. Ap. '21. Kuklux Klan revived. Frank Parker Stockbridge.

Harper's Weekly. 52: 14-16. F. 8, '08. Ku Klux Klan of today: the red record of Kentucky's night riders. Charles V. Tevis.

Literary Digest. 68: 44-6. F. 5, '21. Imperial wizard and his Klan.

Literary Digest. 70: 12-13. Ag. 27, '21. Reign of the tar-bucket.

Literary Digest. 70: 34-40. S. 24, '21. For and against the Ku Klux Klan.
Literary Digest. 74: 14. Ag. 5, '22. Ku Klux victory in Texas.
Literary Digest. 74: 44-52. Ag. 5, '22. Quaint customs and methods of the Ku Klux Klan.
Literary Digest. 75: 13. N. 11, '22. Why Kansas bans the Klan.
Literary Digest. 75: 12-13. D. 2, '22. Klan as a national problem.
Literary Digest. 76: 20-1. F. 3, '23. Canada's keep-out to Klanism.
Metropolitan Magazine. 22: 657-69. S. '05. Story of the Ku Klux Klan. Thomas Dixon, Jr.
Mississippi Valley Historical Review. 1: 575-8. Mr. '15. Ku Klux document. Walter L. Fleming.
Nation. 115: 654. D. 13, '22. Even the Klan has rights.
Nation. 116: 6. Ja. 3, '23. Solemn but undignified pequins.
New Republic. 33: 289. F. 7, '23. Why of the Ku Klux Klan. Mary W. Herring.
Outlook. 132: 643. D. 13, '22. Invisible government.
Spectator. 130: 279-80. F. 17, '23. Ku Klux Klan in America. Frank R. Kent.
Survey. 48: 10-11, 42-3. Ap. 1-8, '22. Klan in Texas. Edward T. Devine.
Texas State Historical Association Quarterly. 9: 262-8. Ap. '06. Ku Klux Klan. W. D. Wood.
Wide World Magazine. 47: 339-47. Ag. '21. K.K.K.: the strongest secret society on earth. Shaw Desmond.
World's Work. 44: 296-302. Jl. '22. Midsummer politics and primaries. Mark Sullivan.

Affirmative References

A B C of the Knights of the Ku Klux Klan. 8p. Ku Klux Press, Atlanta, Ga.

Burton, Annie Cooper. Ku Klux Klan. 38p. Warren T. Potter, Los Angeles. 1916.

Literary Digest. 76: 18-19. Ja. 20, '23. Defense of the Ku Klux Klan.

Mahoney, William James. Some ideals of the Ku Klux Klan. 8p. Knights of the Ku Klux Klan, Atlanta, Ga.

Sawyer, R. H. Truth about the Invisible empire, Knights of the Ku Klux Klan. 16p. Pacific Northwest Domain, 326 Pittock Building, Portland, Oregon. 1922.
<small>The author asserts material change of mind since pamphlet was published.</small>

Simmons, William Joseph. Ku Klux Klan. 12p. Author, Atlanta, Ga.

Negative References

Atlantic Monthly. 130: 122-8. Jl. '22. Modern Ku Klux Klan. Leroy Percy.

City Record. (Boston). 15: 93. Ja. 17, '23. Mayor Curley's ringing letter on Ku Klux Klan.

Congressional Record. (Current). 62: 14207-18. S. 22, '22. Against Ku Klux Klan—for religious liberty. Walter M. Chandler.

Congressional Record. 63: 13-14. N. 21, '22. Alleged outrages in Louisiana.

Current Opinion. 71: 561-4. N. '21. Invisible empire in the spotlight.

Forum. 65: 426-34. Ap. '21. Reviving the Ku Klux Klan. Walter F. White.

Fry, Henry P. Modern Ku Klux Klan. 259p. $2. Small, Maynard, Boston. 1923.
<small>Contains same material as the expose of the New York World in 1921.</small>

Gillis, James M. Ku Klux Klan. 14p. 5c. Paulist Press, 120 W. 60 St, New York. 1922.

Independent. 109: 333-4. D. 9, '22. Collapse of constitutional government. Chester T. Crowell.
<small>Political activities in Texas.</small>

Leslie's Illustrated Weekly. 133: 329-30, 508-11. S. 10, O. 15, '21. Nightgown tyranny; Fighting the K.K.K. on its home grounds. William G. Shepherd.

KU KLUX KLAN

Literary Digest. 70:30-1. O. 1, '21. Ku Klux condemned by the religious press.

Literary Digest. 73:15. Je. 10, '22. Ku Klux in politics.

Literary Digest. 75:33. N. 25, '22. Protestants disowning the Ku Klux Klan.

Literary Digest. 75:31-2. D. 23, '22. New York's anti-Klan outburst.

Literary Digest. 76:10-12. Ja. 13, '23. Murders of Mer Rouge.

Nation. 113:285-6. S. 14, '21. Ku Klux Klan—soul of chivalry. Albert de Silver.
<small>Reprinted by American Civil Liberties Union, 138 W. 13 St. New York. 7p. 2c.</small>

Nation. 115:8-10. Jl. 5, '22. Great bigotry merger. Charles P. Sweeney.

Nation. 115:514. N. 15, '22. Our own secret fascisti.

Nation's peril. 144p. Friends of the compiler. New York. 1872.

New Republic. 25:195-7. Ja. 12, '21. Election by terror in Florida.

New Republic. 28:88-9. S. 21, '21. K.K.K.

New Republic. 33:189-90. Ja. 17, '23. Ku Klux and crime.

New Statesman. 18:40-2. O. 15. '21. K.K.K.—the white terror of America.

New York Times. (Sports Sec.) D. 7, '22. Starts nation-wide fight on Klan here.
<small>Work of the American Unity League.</small>

New York World. Facts about the Ku Klux Klan as the World told them. 16p. New York. 1921.

Outlook. 129:46. S. 14, '21. Imperial lawlessness.

Outlook. 129:79-80. S. 21, '21. Ku Klux Klan again.

Survey. 48:251-2. My. 13, '22. Ku Klux Klan. Edward T. Ware, A. Texan, and Edward T. Devine.

Survey. 49:76-7. O. 15, '22. Intolerance in Oregon.

Witcher, W. C. Unveiling of the Ku Klux Klan. 62p. 50c. Author, Fort Worth, Texas. 1922.

Later References

Atlantic Monthly. 132: 586-92. N. '23. Klan and the church in Indiana. L. Mellett.

Century. 105: 873-82. Ap. '23. Ku Klux Klan, its social origin in the south. F. Tannenbaum.

Collier's. 72: 12. N. 3, '23. Texan challenges the Klan. M. Bentley.

Literary Digest. 80: 36-40. Mr. 8, '24. Colonel Simmons and $146,000, from K.K.K. to K.F.S.

Mecklin, John Moffatt. Ku Klux Klan: a study of the American mind. 244p. Harcourt. New York. 1924.

Nation. 117: 570. N. 21, '23. Klan and the bottle.

New Republic. 35: 67-9. Je. 13, '23. Klan on trial. A. I. Harris.

New Republic. 36: 321-2. N. 21, '23. Why they join the Klan.

New Republic. 37: 44. D. 5, '23. Defence of the Klan. C. M. Rork.

New Statesman. 22: 135-6. N. 10, '23. K.K.K. again.

North American Review. 219: 1-7. Ja. '24. Know nothing and Ku Klux Klan. W. S. Myers.

Outlook. 134: 109. Je. 6, '23. Law for others, not for the Ku Klux Klan!

Outlook. 135: 438-40. N. 14, '23. Night-riding reformers. S. Frost.

Outlook. 135: 530-1. N. 28, '23. Klan, the king, and a revolution. S. Frost.

Outlook. 135: 674-6, 716-18; 136: 20-4, 64-6, 100-3, 144-7, 183-6, 217-19, 261-4, 308-11, 350-3. D. 19, '23-F. 27, '24. When the Klan rules. S. Frost.

World Tomorrow. 7: 74-87. Mr. '24. Ku Klux Klan.

World's Work. 46: 31-8, 174-83. My.-Je. '23. Salesmen of hate: the Ku Klux Klan. R. L. Duffus.

World's Work. 46: 363-72. Ag. '23. Ku Klux Klan in the middle west. R. L. Duffus.

World's Work. 46: 527-36. S. '23. Ancestry and the end of the Ku Klux Klan. R. L. Duffus.

REPRINTS

KU KLUX KLAN REVIVAL[1]

The Ku Klux Klan crossed Mason and Dixon's line in the winter of 1920-21. Revived in the south some five years ago, this secret, oath-bound organization that had its origin in the troublous times of the reconstruction period following the Civil War in America, began during the winter just past to extend its activities into the north and west, with the avowed intention of uniting native-born white Christians for concerted action in the preservation of American institutions and the supremacy of the white race.

In New York City and in other centers even further distant from the region in which the original Ku Klux Klan was active there have been planted nuclei of the revived organization, according to the statements of its officials. How many such centers have been established in the north and west and the extent of the membership are not revealed. As in the original Ku Klux Klan, members are known only to each other; the general public is permitted to know only certain national officers connected with the organization.

To the average American the mention of the name suggests terrorism. The mental picture of the Ku Klux, to those to whom the words conjure up any mental picture at all, is of a band of white-robed, hooded riders, appearing mysteriously out of the darkness and proceeding, silently and with complete discipline, to execute some extra-legal mission of warning or of private vengeance. That, at least, is the reaction of the average northern

[1] By Frank Parker Stockbridge. Current History Magazine, New York Times. 14 : 19-25. April, 1921.

white man, whose knowledge of the Ku Klux Klan is derived entirely from reading or the "movies." To him it is something like the Vigilantes of early California days or the "Night Riders" of the Kentucky tobacco war of the early twentieth century; the words carry to his ears an unmistakable flavor of lynch law, and, if he be old enough to have read the writings of Albion W. Tourgée and other northern authors who wrote of the south in the reconstruction period, he cannot escape the implication of lawless oppression of the negro by the white.

Attitude of the North

That substantially the impression set down above is that prevailing in the north, where any impression of the Ku Klux Klan at all exists, is probably a conservative statement of the fact. It was doubtless such an impression that led the mayor of New York to declare, in a public letter, that the entrance of the Ku Klux Klan into the metropolis would not be tolerated. An assistant district attorney, Alfred J. Talley, since elevated to the bench of the General Sessions, took occasion in the autumn of 1920, when it was stated in newspaper dispatches that the Klan was about to extend its organization into the north, to write a letter to the newspapers declaring that any attempt on the part of the Ku Klux to carry on in the county of New York what he regarded as its customary activities would be the signal for action by the criminal authorities of the county. Mr. Talley undoubtedly voiced the general northern view, at that time, of the Ku Klux Klan.

Alfred J. Talley, Assistant District Attorney of New York, when informed of the effort to organize a Ku Klux Klan in New York City, expressed himself as follows:

There is no room in the great, broadminded state of New York for so un-American an organization as the Ku Klux Klan. The pretension that it apparently makes to patriotism enforces Samuel Johnson's definition of patriotism, "The last refuge of a scoundrel." No secret oath-bound organization is needed to preserve and perpetuate devotion to the American government, nor to uphold the laws of the land, and the Constitution upon which our government is founded.

Mr. Talley referred to the organization as composed of "narrow-minded bigots" and "scareheaded fanatics, who are opposed to everything that Abraham Lincoln stood for.

There is no place for them in New York, and the citizens and real Americans will set their faces against them and their wild aspirations.

When this announcement was published on December 17, 1920, William Joseph Simmons of Atlanta, Ga., styling himself "Imperial Wizard of the Ku Klux Klan," telegraphed Mr. Talley, asking him whether he had been correctly quoted, whereupon Mr. Talley sent this reply:

I was correctly quoted, and my remarks were directed specifically at your organization.

As Viewed in the South

To the southern white man, however, the name of this organization brings up a different picture.

"The Ku Klux Klan saved the south" is the expression in which he sums up in a phrase a point of view which has grown into a fixed tradition in the states of the former Confederacy. To the average southern white man of today the name of the Ku Klux Klan, after the lapse of half a century, typifies all that was best and finest in the chivalry of the old south. It conveys to him the impression of valiant men resisting tyranny, of the salvation of the white race from threatened negro domination (with all that that implied socially as well as politically), and of the rescue of the white womanhood of the south from a frightful and ever-present peril.

The purpose of the Ku Klux Klan has been sympathetically recorded by Dr. Walter Lynwood Fleming, Professor of History in the Vanderbilt University, who edited Lester and Wilson's "History of the Ku Klux

Klan" and is the author of several historical books and articles dealing with the reconstruction period.

"The object [of the Ku Klux Klan] was to protect the whites during the disorders that followed the Civil War, and to oppose the policy of the north toward the south," says Dr. Fleming in an article in the Encyclopaedia Britannica. "The result of the whole movement was a more or less successful revolution against the reconstruction and an overthrow of the governments based on negro suffrage."

Origin of the Order

Formed in 1865 at Pulaski, Tenn., as a social club of young white men, with what Dr. Fleming calls "an absurd ritual and a strange uniform," it was soon discovered by the members that "the fear of it had a great influence over the lawless but superstitious blacks." In the difficult situation confronting the conquered south, it was inevitable that this power to terrorize should be availed of. "Soon," says Dr. Fleming, "the club expanded into a great federation of regulators, absorbing numerous local bodies that had been formed in the absence of civil law and partaking of the nature of the old English neighborhood police and the ante-bellum slave patrol."

Among the conditions and causes that enabled the Ku Klux Klan to develop in two or three years into the most powerful instrument of regulation in the whole south, Dr. Fleming enumerates these:

"The absence of stable government in the south for several years after the Civil War; the corrupt and tyrannical rule of the alien, renegade and negro; the disfranchisement of whites; the spread of ideas of social and political equality among the negroes; fear of negro insurrections; the arming of the negro militia and the disarming of whites; outrages upon white women by black men; the influence of northern adventurers in the Freedmen's

Bureau and the Union League in alienating the races; the humiliation of Confederate soldiers after they had been paroled—in general, the insecurity felt by southern whites during the decade after the collapse of the Confederacy."

"The Invisible Empire"

In its perfect organization the old Ku Klux Klan had at its head, with the title of Grand Wizard, General Nathan Bedford Forrest, the former Confederate cavalry leader whom General William Tecumseh Sherman characterized as "the most remarkable man the Civil War produced on either side." The Grand Wizard ruled the "Invisible Empire," which consisted of the entire south. Over each state or "realm" presided a "Grand Dragon." Counties were "provinces," each with its "Grand Giant"; a group of counties was a "Dominion" ruled by a "Grand Titan" and local units were "dens," over which the "Grand Cyclops" held sway. Staff officers bore such titles as Genii, Hydras, Furies, Goblins, Night Hawks, Magi, Monks and Turks, while individual members were Ghouls.

The constitution of the Ku Klux Klan, like that of the similar though larger organization, the Knights of the White Camelia and several smaller groups having the same general purposes, contained certain declarations of principles which Professor Fleming thus summarizes:

To protect and succor the weak and unfortunate, especially the widows and orphans of Confederate soldiers; to protect members of the white race in life, honor and property from the encroachments of the blacks; to oppose the Radical Republican Party and the Union League; to defend constitutional liberty, to prevent usurpation, to emancipate the whites, maintain peace and order, the laws of God, the principles of 1776 and the political and social supremacy of the white race—in short, to oppose African influence in government and society and to prevent any intermingling of the races.

Native whites, largely disfranchised because of their active participation in the rebellion, formed one moiety of the social structure of the south at the close of the

Civil War; the other part was composed of the newly enfranchised blacks, the northern white man (called "carpet-baggers") who participated in the effort to set up a negro government in the southern states and a modicum of native whites who cooperated with them, known as "scalawags." The Ku Klux movement was an effort of the first class to destroy the control of the second class.

Some of the Methods

Professor Fleming says:

> To control the negro, the Klan played upon his superstitious fears by having night patrols, parades and drills of silent horsemen covered with white sheets, carrying skulls with coals of fire for eyes, sacks of bones to rattle and wearing hideous masks. . . Mysterious signs and warnings were sent to disorderly negro politicians. The whites who were responsible for the conduct of the blacks were warned or driven away by social or business ostracism or by violence. Nearly all southern whites . . . took part in the Ku Klux movement. As the work of the societies succeeded they gradually passed out of existence. In some communities they fell into the control of violent men and became simply bands of outlaws . . . and the anarchical aspects of the movement excited the north to vigorous condemnation.

The United States Congress in 1871-72 enacted laws intended to break up the Ku Klux and other secret societies; several hundred arrests were made and several convictions followed. Much of the violence was checked, but the movement undoubtedly accomplished its prime purposes of giving protection to the whites, reducing the blacks to order, driving out the "carpet-baggers" and nullifying the laws that had placed the southern whites under control of the party of the former slaves.

It is easy to see from the above sketch whence both the northerner and the southerner derive their contrary impressions of the organization. The former remembers the congressional investigations and trials of the Ku Klux leaders, the evidence adduced of violence and law-breaking, of the whipping of negroes and of carpet-baggers and even of men being dragged from their beds and slain;

the latter remembers, or has had handed down to him the story of the time when, to quote from Woodrow Wilson's "History of the American People," "adventurers swarmed out of the north, as much the enemies of one race as of the other, to cozen, beguile and use the negroes. The white men were aroused by a mere instinct of self-preservation—until at last there sprung into existence a great Ku Klux Klan, a veritable empire of the south, to protect the southern country."

That the occasion which gave rise to the original Ku Klux movement was a real crisis, affecting the welfare and happiness of a whole people, the impartial historian of today may well concede; that in meeting the crisis by the means that were used the south was fighting for the preservation of what it deemed right, even holy, with the only weapon at its command, is hardly to be controverted.

Ku Klux Klan Today

What crisis, what menace to the ideals and the civilization of any considerable body of people exists today to give vitality to the revival of the Ku Klux Klan after the lapse of fifty years? Unless some satisfying answer can be made to that question, the subject is hardly one to be treated seriously; unless there exists (or it is believed by a great number of persons that there does exist) a real need for the banding together of native-born white Christians in a militant organization for mutual protection, any organization based on such a premise must inevitably fall to pieces of its own weight. And while the original Ku Klux Klan was purely sectional in its activities, whereas the revived Ku Klux Klan is extending its field to the entire United States, the ground for its existence and continued growth must be sought in national rather than in local conditions.

Part of the answer to the question just propounded is not difficult to deduce from such of the literature of the Ku Klux as is permitted to be distributed to those not affiliated with the organization; part of it is contained in statements by high officials of the organization or published with their sanction.

To every inquirer writing to the Klan's headquarters in Atlanta for information is sent a printed form of questionnaire. Of the twenty questions asked on this paper, which must be filled out and signed before further information is vouchsafed nine seem to be pertinent to the point under consideration. These are:

> Were your parents born in the United States of America?
> Are you a Gentile or a Jew?
> Are you of the white race or of a colored race?
> Do you believe in the principles of a pure Americanism?
> Do you believe in white supremacy?
> What is your politics?
> What is your religious faith?
> Of what religious faith are your parents?
> Do you owe any kind of allegiance to any foreign nation, government, institution, sect, people, ruler or person?

To the inquirer sending in the questionnaire satisfactorily filled out there become available pamphlets giving details of the organization's present purposes and principles. To quote from one of these pamphlets:

> The purpose of the modern Ku Klux Klan is to inculcate the sacred principles and noble ideals of chivalry, the development of character, the protection of the home and the chastity of womanhood, the exemplification of a pure and practical patriotism toward our glorious country, the preservation of American ideals and institutions, and the maintenance of white supremacy. . . Only native-born white American citizens who believe in the tenets of the Christian religion and who owe no allegiance of any degree or nature to any foreign government or institution, religious or political, or to any sect, people or persons, are eligible for membership.

Classes That Are Barred

Five classes of persons are at once barred by this pronouncement. They are: (1) negroes, (2) Japanese and other Orientals, (3) Roman Catholics, (4) Jews, (5) all foreign-born persons.

Without questioning the right of the Ku Klux or of any other organization to set up its own qualifications for membership and to exclude any individual or any group of individuals, it is of interest to note that the four groups particularly excluded in this instance are, each in degree varying with local conditions, the storm-centers of present-day racial antagonisms in the United States.

Anti-Semitic propaganda is more open and active in America than at any time in recent history.

To the mass mind of America the Irish question is chiefly a religious question; the issue at stake the control of Ireland by the Roman Catholic Church, and the persistent effort of the American supporters of Sinn Fein to arouse antagonism in this country toward England a subtle piece of religious propaganda. Quite regardless of its truth or falsity, there can be no doubt of the wide acceptance of this view by a large proportion of Protestant Americans.

That the Japanese question is a tremendously vital issue west of the Rockies is a familiar fact to every newspaper reader; it is equally true that the anti-Japanese sentiment of the Pacific coast is shared by a large proportion of Americans in other sections, who have become convinced that the interests of the nation are seriously menaced by Japanese occupation of California lands and that war with Japan may occur at any time.

The Negro Question

New impetus has been given to the negro question, more particularly in the south, but to some extent throughout the country, by conditions arising from the war. The great demand for labor during the war brought about the greatest migration in history of negroes from the south to the north. High wages, north and south, raised the negro for a time to unheard-of pinnacles of affluence. Then the sudden slump in business threw back into idleness thousands who had become accustomed to "easy money." Many of these found themselves hundreds of miles from their homes with no means of returning; large fractions of the whole number had forgotten their old habit of docility in their brief period of financial independence and ventured to assert their rights as citizens in a manner offensive to the dominant white race.

Renewed agitation for the recognition of the negro on the plane of complete equality with the whites was one of the inevitable results of the war conditions that put the negro worker on the same economic plane with the white workman; the negro soldier and officer into the same uniform and the same service as the white soldier. The demands of the National Association for the Advancement of the Colored People for the abolition of segregation of the races in the government departments at Washington, the reduction of Congressional representation in the southern states in proportion as the negro is disfranchised, the pardon of the imprisoned soldiers of the Twenty-fourth Infantry held in Leavenworth for the Houston riots, the abolition of "Jim Crow" cars on interstate railroad trains and the appointment of negro Assistant Secretaries of Labor and Agriculture are pointed to by officials of the Ku Klux Klan as proof that white supremacy is now acutely and nationally menaced. The National Association for the Advancement of Colored People, in turn, has included in its published statement of purposes "The defeat, by every legitimate means, of the nefarious Ku Klux Klan, both south and north." So the issue here, at least, is squarely joined.

National Expansion Sought

It is on such grounds as those just enumerated that the revived Ku Klux Klan bases its expectation of extending beyond the boundaries of the south. It has been in existence, this present-day successor of the old Ku Klux, since the latter part of 1915, when it was chartered as a legitimate fraternal organization by the state of Georgia. The originator of the idea of reviving the old institution under the old name was Colonel William Joseph Simmons of Atlanta, now Professor of Southern History in Lanier University. Associated with him in the application for a charter from the state of Georgia were three surviving members of the old Ku Klux Klan. By virtue of this fact the new Klan declares itself, in its constitution, to be the only legitimate heir of the original organization, with sole rights to all its signs, symbols, regalias, etc. It is organized on similar lines to the original Ku Klux Klan, with similar, though slightly different, titles for its officers. Colonel Simmons is the "Imperial Wizard" or supreme head of the order, the full title of which is "The Invisible Empire, Knights of the Ku Klux Klan." The old regalia of white robe and pointed cap covering the face of the wearer is retained by the new organization, which claims to be fully organized throughout the south and to have a considerable number of local nuclei planted in half or more of the states.

Pretends to Uphold Law

Cooperation with the authorities of the law is set forth as one of the tenets of the revived Ku Klux Klan. "Because certain individuals at various times have committed acts of violence under cover of darkness and shielded by masks and robes somewhat resembling the official regalia of the Ku Klux Klan," says one of the organization's official pronouncements, "they have been classed as members of this organization. The Ku Klux Klan is a strictly law-abiding organization, and every member is sworn to uphold the law at all times and to assist officers of the law in preserving peace and order whenever the occasion may arise, and any member violating this oath would be banished forever from the organization.

Among the principles for which this organization stands are: Suppression of graft by public office holders;

preventing the causes of mob violence and lynchings; preventing unwarranted strikes by foreign agitators; sensible and patriotic immigration laws; sovereignty of state rights under the Constitution; separation of church and state, and freedom of speech and press, a freedom such as does not strike at nor imperil our government or the cherished institutions of our people."

Among the membership of the old Ku Klux Klan were many northern soldiers, members of the army of occupation sent into the south after the Civil War to preserve order and maintain the reconstruction governments in power. In the new Ku Klux Klan, it is stated, are to be found state, county and municipal officials of every degree, police officers and men, as well as a number of United States officials, Senators and members of Congress.

One Instance of Operations

How the Klan operates may best be indicated by quoting from statements publicly made by authority of its national officials. Birmingham, Ala., recently had a "wave of crime." The Ku Klux Klan offered its services to the city officials to help stamp out evil conditions. The offer was accepted, and the seven hundred local members directed their efforts, in secret, against criminals and "undesirables" of both races. Their claim that they rendered valuable assistance to the police is supported by the fact that they assert that the Chief of Police of Birmingham sent a telegram to the Chief of Police of Nashville, Tenn., when he learned that a branch of the organization was to be established there, heartily endorsing the Ku Klux movement. They claim that many such letters and telegrams of endorsement from mayors, sheriffs and chiefs of police of southern cities are on file in the Klan's headquarters.

In Jacksonville, Fla., the method of a public parade at night was adopted. Several hundred members of the

Klan, garbed in robes and hoods, rode through the city, scattering printed placards which read:

WARNING—UNDESIRABLES, BOTH WHITE AND BLACK, WE KNOW YOU. THIS LOAFING, THIEVING AND PROWLING AROUND MUST STOP.
KNIGHTS OF THE KU KLUX KLAN.

A high official of the Ku Klux Klan told the writer of a dramatic though less spectacular demonstration of the organization's methods. He stated that in one city, in which it was well organized, an investigation into underlying conditions making for crime and disorder indicated that the chief trouble lay in the manner in which one of the city's courts was conducted. A special committee, he says, with an expert investigator employed, spent weeks in drawing up what amounted to an indictment of the judge of this court. The document was handed to the judge with a letter, signed by the Ku Klux Klan, asking him to read the charges and to realize that his future course would be as carefully scrutinized as his past actions. He stated there was no threat, no demand for his resignation; on the contrary, the belief was expressed that he could and would reform the conditions in his court. "A year later," said the official who told this story, "I was talking with a very eminent jurist who was familiar with the conditions in this court. He said that the improvement that had been observed in its conduct had been a matter of the greatest gratification to him, and that he had been unable to account for it until I told him how it was brought about."

The power of the Ku Klux Klan today, like that of its prototype of half a century ago, lies in the secrecy and mystery with which it and its operations are surrounded. Its members are known only to each other and may not disclose the fact of their membership to outsiders. Outside the Klan none can know whether its warnings are backed by ten men or thousands in any community. To the assertion that there is no need and no room for such an extra-legal institution to enforce law and order, the officers of the Klan point to the newspaper chronicles of crime and disorder in every part of the country. To the charge that they are a negro-whipping organization, thriving on race prejudice, they reply that no law-abiding person of any race, creed or color has anything to fear from them; they assert that they are the friends of every self-respecting man, black or white, but that they maintain the inherent superiority of the Caucasian stock, and that their order intends to use every legitimate means to retain it in control of America.

KU KLUX KLAN—WHO—WHY—WHAT [1]

The history of civilization has many instances in which a race, religious or class consciousness has come and swept all before it, and often these revolutions of thought have found expression in secret orders.

The Maccabeans, the early Christians, the Crusaders, the Reformation, the French Revolution, Cromwell's Commonwealth, the Boston Tea Party and many other great solvents in civilization were only able to effectively oppose the establishment of, or throw off the yoke of, tyranny by shrouding their work in secrecy during the movement's early stages.

Among the great secret movements of the world's history that have been brought into existence to right the wrongs of humanity, there is no more shining example than the original, genuine order of the Ku Klux Klan which was organized in 1866, and after accomplishing its noble purpose, *voluntarily* disbanded by order of its Grand Wizard, General Nathan Bedford Forrest, in the year 1870.

The *Ku Klux Klan*—The Invisible Empire—was the great idea of American reconstruction. We say "American reconstruction" for the reason that all America was affected by reconstruction influences. The south most of all, yes, but nevertheless—*all;* for the great threat to the white race that loomed on the horizon of the south would

[1] From A B C of the Ku Klux Klan. Ku Klux Klan Press, Atlanta, Georgia.

have spread throughout the entire nation, had not the white robe of the Ku Klux Klan kept unrevealed those courageous and devoted hearts that were consecrated to saving the Anglo-Saxon civilization of our country, protecting the homes and well-being of our people and shielding the virtue of womanhood.

The original Ku Klux were *not outlaws* or *moral degenerates*, nor did they perpetrate outlawry. They were men of moral and social standing and their leaders were men of sterling character and unquestioned culture. They reverently bowed to the soul of real *law* and swore to enforce its principle of justice, protection and the pursuit of happiness. Their strong arm fought valiantly for the preservation of the integrity of the race against the cruelty of base, unjust and tyrannical legislation and insufferable conditions created by a horde of conscienceless, diabolical, greed and lust-crazed adventurers that swarmed down from the north to use the negro for their own damnable, selfish ends. These adventurers poisoned the minds of and brutalized the inoffensive negro and converted many of them into human beasts by their cheap whisky and glaring promises of rich reward and loosed them armed and inflamed upon the sacred privileges and persons of the suffering and defenseless southern people.

The Ku Klux Klan stood firmly upon the solemn promise of the federal government made through General Grant to General Lee, and the rights of citizens vouchsafed by the Constitution and it swore allegiance to the principles of that Constitution. It was the defender of justice, the enforcer of civil and racial law and the great regulator of the galling irregularities of prostituted law at the hands of so-called men, the mentioning of whose names is an insult to the blood of the race of Caucasian stock. It struck from the neck of the wounded, bleeding, pauperized and prostrated south the dirty heel of the degenerated *outlaw*—the "scalawag" and the "carpet-bagger" and the misguided, lust-crazed negro, and made possible the birth of the greatest nation of all time —the re-United States of America; it destroyed the fanatic's vile hope of the amalgamation of the races, firmly established the most valuable heritage of the race—white supremacy—forever, and restored the people of Washington, Jefferson, Marion and their compatriots in the founding of the nation to their rightful place in the peerless pleasure of American citizenship.

In all history no people has ever suffered such torturous humiliation and endured such intense woe as the people of the south during the frightful night of the American reconstruction, and God only knows what the ultimate result would have been had the atrocious reconstruction scheme of those contemptible politicians who conceived and engineered it gone on to a successful consummation.

The most vicious and deadly enemies of both races were the dirty carpet-bagger and his vile henchmen—the scalawag—who together controlled the Freedman's Bureau and other organizations and perpetrated the most abominable outrages on humanity known in the annals of civilization. They had at their beck and call the combined powers of a great nation well trained in arms, and detachments of troops were in every county in the south. By them the law and the Constitution were regarded as "mere scraps of paper"; for, under the so-called martial law the whim and word of every petty military commandant was *enforced* and no one dared to question, dispute or complain. No man's home was safe, the chastity of womankind was not secure, and the property right of the people was a thing of the past.

This was the terrible condition, unparalleled in history, which was ruthlessly imposed upon the southern people. The devil and his most infamous imps held undisputed sway. The night was dark; for all the stars had gone out. To correct this condition and to break the greedy grasp of this unutterable tyranny called for mystery and action; mystery complete, and action drastic, courageous, certain, swift and sure. In the providence of God the Ku Klux Klan arose, a mighty impulse of an unconquered race, a veritable and invisible empire to save the southern country and to destroy an organized force of diabolism that threatened the whole nation.

The work of that mystic society was indeed well done. It met the combined force against it and through many years of dangerous and strenuous strife it won, and in winning it brought order out of chaos, replaced fanatical, pernicious persecution with perpetual peace; the wail of poverty with the music of prosperity; insolent indolence with industry and thrift, and compelled the whole world to recognize the racial barriers erected by the Creator of races and preserved from an everlasting legalized contamination the sacred blood of the Caucasian race. Through it right triumphed over might; an unscrupulous military dictatorship was forever removed, Constitutional law was re-enthroned, righteous justice was re-established among men and the sovereign rights of the people respected. It did more toward cementing anew the alienated states of our nation into an indissoluble Union than any other organized force. It harbored no prejudice and perpetrated no injustices; it committed no malicious wrong and accomplished its intricate, titanic task and achieved its noble mission and purpose "without fear and without reproach."

A greater achievement in all history was never accomplished for culture, civilization and humanity. The men of that society were the champions of real liberty and the peerless paragons of a pure patriotism. A great courage, a dauntless spirit, a manly, *necessary* mission and lofty ideals were the actuating principles of those valiant men.

The Ku Klux Klan by its unselfish, patriotic achievement stands pre-eminent as the greatest order of real chivalry the world has ever known, and its members were the noblest heroes in the great world's history. In simple justice should their sacred memory be forgotten? Should their patriotic achievements be lost to posterity?

Shall we of this and those of future generations allow the cruel calumny, satanic slander and flagrant falsehoods heaped upon them for the past half-century to pass, be repeated and go unanswered by an accurate and honest revelation of the whole *truth,* and suffer our progeny to believe that they are under disgrace by being descendants of a degraded and beastly ancestry? *No! No!! No!!!* No *real* man in all America will consent to such a crime against the heroic dead. Hence, a great *memorial* is now being built to commemorate those men and perpetuate their spiritual purpose and ideals. This *monument* shall be constructed of *real* American manhood and cast in the proportions and character of a great fraternal order and it is and shall be known as the

Invisible Empire
Knights of the Ku Klux Klan

The noble ride of the Ku Klux Klan is immortalized by their accomplishments, and is memorialized by the men of today who appreciate the chivalric, holy and patriotic achievements of the original Klan in the permanence of *this* great fraternity. The spirit of the Ku Klux Klan still lives, and should live a priceless heritage to be sacredly treasured by all those who love their country, regardless of section, and are proud of its sacred traditions. That this spirit may live always to warm the hearts of manly men, unify them by the spirit of a holy clanishness, to assuage the billowing tide of fraternal alienation that surges in human breasts, and inspire them to achieve the highest and noblest in the defense of our country, our race, our homes, each other and humanity is the *paramount ideal* of the Knights of the Ku Klux Klan—a great institution composed of men of character and intelligence, men who aspire to that which is noble for themselves and humanity.

A few survivors of the old Klan were among the charter members of the Knights of the Ku Klux Klan, and old Klansmen who can qualify are taken into the order without cost and shall be known as "Klansmen-Emeritus," or "Original Klansmen," for they are worthy.

A Sacred Duty—A Precious Privilege

A true American cannot give a higher and more sincere expression of appreciation of and gratitude for what was accomplished by our fathers in the defense of home and the sacred rights of our people than by becoming a "citizen of the Invisible Empire, Knights of the Ku Klux Klan." He cannot align himself with any institution that will mean so much for himself, his home and his country as this great order.

It Stands For

A America first: First in thought, first in affections and first in the galaxy of nations. The stars and stripes forever above all other and every kind of government in the whole world.

B Benevolence: In thought, word and deed based upon justice and practically applied to all. To right the wrong; to succor the weak and unfortunate; to help the worthy and to relieve the distressed.

C Clanishness: Real fraternity practically applied—standing by and sticking to each other in all things honorable. Encouraging, protecting, cultivating and exemplifying the real "fraternal human relationship" to shield and enhance each other's happiness and welfare. A devoted, unfailing loyalty to the principles, mission and purposes of the order in promoting the highest and best interest of the community, state and nation.

What it is: It is a *standard fraternal order* enforcing fraternal conduct, and not merely a "social association." It is a duly incorporated, legally recognized institution, honest in purpose, made in sentiment and practical in results that commands the hearty respect of all respectable people throughout the nation. It is not encouraging or condoning any propaganda of religious intolerance nor racial prejudice. It is an association of *real* men who believe in *being* something, in doing things worth while and who are in *all things* 100 *per cent pure* American. Yet it is vastly more than merely a social fraternal order.

Its initial purpose: An enduring monument to the valor and patriotic achievements of the Ku Klux Klan. That this monument be not embodied in cold, emotionless stone, but in living, pulsating human hearts and active human brains, and find a useful expression in the nobility of the character of real manly men; this is the only memorial that will adequately befit the memory of the valiant Ku Klux Klan.

Its lineage: The most sublime lineage in history, commemorating and perpetuating, as it does, the most dauntless organization known to man.

Its secret: Sacred guardianship to the most sacred cause.

Its courage: The soul of chivalry and virtue's impenetrable shield. The impulse of an unconquered race.

Its teachings: To inculcate the sacred principles and noble ideals of the world's greatest order of chivalry; and direct the way of the initiate through the veil of mystic philosophy into the Empire Invisible.

Its character: The noblest concepts of manhood idealized in thought and materialized in practice in all the relationships of life. Mystery and action; mastery and achievement.

Its ritualism: Is vastly different from anything in the whole universe of fraternal ritualism. It is altogether original, weird, mystical and of a high class, leading up through four degrees. Dignity and decency are its marked features. It unfolds a spiritual philosophy that has to do with the very fundamentals of life and living, here and hereafter. He who explores the dismal depths of the mystic cave and from thence attains the lofty heights of superior knighthood may sit among the gods in the Empire Invisible.

Its patriotism: An uncompromising standard of pure Americanism untrammeled by alien influences and free from the entanglements of foreign alliances. Proclaiming the brotherhood of nations but wedding none, thereby unyielding in the dignity of our own independence and forever faultless in our freedom.

Its mission: Duty—without fault, without fail, without fear and without reproach.

Its society: The practical fraternal fellowship of men whose standard is worth not wealth; character, not cash, courageous manhood based upon honor untarnished by the touch of hypocrisy or the veneering of society's selfish social valuations.

Its place: In the heart of every "true American," alongside of every other fraternal order, and in its original casting, unique mannerism, sacred sentiment, noble purpose and peculiar mysticism it is separate and apart from any and all and peerless in its distinctive peculiarities.

Its fraternity: Not merely reciting in ceremony pretty, time-worn platitudes on brotherly love, but to enforce a fraternal practice of *clanishness;* thereby making devotion to its standard worth while. "The glory of a Klansman is to serve."

Its origin: This great institution, as a patriotic, ritualistic fraternal order, is no hastily "jumped-up" affair. It has been in the making for the past twenty years. It is a product of deliberate thought. The one man (William Joseph Simmons) who is responsible for it conceived the idea twenty years ago. For fourteen years he thought, studied and worked to prepare himself for its launching. He had dedicated his life to this noble cause. He kept his own counsel during these years and in the silent recesses of his soul he thought out the great plan. During the early days of October, 1915, he mentioned his ambition to some friends, among whom were three men who were bona-fide members of the original Klan when it disbanded, they most heartily cooperated with him. Having met with such encouragement he invited several of his friends to a meeting on the night of October 26th, 1915, at which time he unfolded his plans, and as a result all present, thirty-four in number, signed a petition for a charter. The petition was accepted and on Thanksgiving night, 1915, men were seen emerging from the shadows and gathering around the spring at the base of Stone Mountain (the world's greatest rock, near Atlanta, Ga.) and from thence repaired to the mountain top and there under a blazing fiery cross, they took the oath of allegiance to the Invisible Empire, Knights of the Ku Klux Klan. The charter was issued by the state of Georgia, December 4th, 1915, and signed by Honorable Philip Cook, Secretary of State. In the development of the order a petition was made to the Superior Court, Fulton County, Georgia, for a special charter, and said charter was issued July 1st, 1916. The Imperial Wizard issued his Imperial Proclamation July 4th, 1916.

And thus on the mountain top that night at the midnight hour while men braved the surging blasts of wild wintry mountain winds and endured a temperature far below freezing, bathed in the sacred glow of the fiery cross, the Invisible Empire was called from its slumber of half a century to take up a new task and fulfill a new mission for humanity's good and to call back to mortal habitation the good angel of practical fraternity among men.

Prerequisites to Citizenship in the Invisible Empire

This order is founded upon dependable character. It is not an ultra-exclusive institution, but its membership is composed of "picked" men.

No man is wanted in this order who hasn't manhood enough to assume a real *oath* with serious purpose to keep the same inviolate.

No man is wanted in this order who will not or cannot swear an unqualified allegiance to the government of the United States of America, its flag and its Constitution.

No man is wanted in this order who does not esteem the government of the United States above any other government, civil, political or ecclesiastical, in the whole world.

No man is wanted in this order who cannot practice *real* fraternity toward each and every one of his oath-bound associates.

Only native-born American citizens who believe in the tenets of the Christian religion and owe no allegiance of any degree or nature to any foreign government, nation, political institution, sect, people or person, are eligible.

Because certain individuals at various times have committed acts of violence under cover of darkness and shielded by masks and robes somewhat resembling the official regalia of the Ku Klux Klan, they have been classed as members of this organization. The Ku Klux Klan is a strictly law-abiding organization and every member is sworn to uphold the law in preserving peace and order whenever the occasion may arise, and any member violating this oath would be banished forever from the organization. In other words, it is a practical fraternal order pledged to wholesome service, and not merely a flashy social association.

Among the principles for which this organization stands, in addition to those already enumerated, are: suppression of graft by public officeholders; preventing the causes of mob-violence and lynching; sensible and patriotic immigration laws; separation of church and state and freedom of speech and press, a freedom of such that does not strike at or imperil our government or the cherished institutions of our people.

If there be any white American citizen who owes allegiance to no flag but the Star Spangled Banner and who cannot subscribe to and support these principles let him forever hold his peace, for he is basely unworthy of the great flag and its government that guarantees to him life, liberty and the pursuit of happiness. That person who actively opposes these great principles is a dangerous ingredient in the body politic of our country and an enemy to the weal of our national commonwealth.

The Ku Klux Klan of today rides on, not upon the backs of faithful steeds, but in the mind, heart and soul of every true white American citizen who loves our great country and who glories in the name America, and who is honest enough as a grateful son to perpetually memoralize the heroism of our fathers and transmit the boon of our priceless heritage untarnished, uncorrupted and unstained to the generations who follow us that the luster of our age may increase in splendor.

The Knights of the Ku Klux Klan, regardless of statements made to the contrary, either through ignorance or with deliberate intent to misrepresent it, has not made, is not now making and does not intend to make any fight on the Roman Catholic church as a religious institution, but it will unalterably and unequivocally oppose any move of the Catholic church or of any other church, individual or organization, which attempts to bring about a combination of church and state in the United States.

The Ku Klux Klan does oppose the attitude of the Catholic church on our public school system, believing that the public schools as an institution should be protected from its enemies regardless of who they may be.

The Ku Klux Klan concedes to every man the right to worship God as he sees fit and in his own way, or to worship Him not at all, and while it adheres strictly to the tenets of the Christian religion it seeks no quarrel with individual or organization because of religious differences.

In its attitude toward the large Jewish population of this country the Knights of the Ku Klux Klan have played square. While its organizers were fully aware that there are thousands of Jewish citizens of the United States whose loyalty to the United States government is unquestioned and who believe in its principles and institutions, it was decided to draw the line because no member of the Jewish faith, after he came into the organization, could be happy or contented with the fellowship he found on the inside for the very simple reason that the entire teaching of the order is that our present civilization rests upon the teachings of Jesus Christ. At every lodge meeting Jesus Christ is lauded and his teachings expounded and the constitution and regulations of the order set forth that the living Christ is the Klanman's criterion of character.

Therefore, even though many Jews could and would qualify for membership in this organization, it would have been unjust to allow the Jew to enter into fellowship with the organization by appealing to his patriotism and then have him cease to attend because every meeting would be out of harmony with his religious convictions.

Thus the organization has deprived itself of a large body of members in its determination to "play the game square" with the Jew as well as the Gentile. We understand that the Jews in this country have their own patriotic organizations, through which loyalty to the United States government, its flag and all that it represents is constantly being instilled into the minds and hearts of the members of their race and with these organizations we are in thorough and hearty accord.

The Ku Klux Klan is not the enemy of the negro. It opposes, and will continue to oppose, the efforts of certain negro organizations and periodicals which are sowing the seeds of discontent and racial hatred among the negroes of this country by preaching and teaching social equality. We believe it is possible for the races to live together in peace and unity only upon condition that each race recognize the rights and privileges of the other. Yet we hold it is obligatory upon the negro race, and upon all other colored races in America to recognize that they are living in the land of the white race and by courtesy of the white race and that the white race cannot be expected to surrender to any other race, either in whole or in part, the control of its vital and fundamental governmental affairs.

There are rights which the negro race and all other colored races have as citizens of this country which the white race—the ruling race—is bound to respect, but they must not, individually or collectively, lose sight of the fact that the white race *is* the ruling race by right of inheritance and that it does not intend to surrender this right or to compromise it with any other race—black, red, yellow or brown.

Let the negro race, and all other races living within our borders, advance and develop and prosper all that they may, but let it be done through their own institutions and within their own race without encroachment upon the rights of other races. Let them understand that in the long run the white man always has proved himself the truest friend and the safest counsellor of all other races in whatever land or clime the races have come in contact and let them not be misled by false prophets who, for personal gain, appeal to their passions and prejudices by wild promises that they know can never be fulfilled.

The Ku Klux Klan is not anti-labor, as is proved by the fact that a large percentage of its membership is composed of union and non-union elements of labor in all parts of the United States. Neither is it anti-capital, unless capital should become tyrannical in its attitude to the government of the United States or the people.

The organization is now extending its membership practically in every state and the combined increase in all states for several months has been approximately one thousand per day.

The expense of the organization work is kept down to the minimum possible cost and all funds of the order are properly and honorably handled in a businesslike way, and the financial records are accurate and complete and subject to inspection at any time by any member or members of the organization. All persons handling funds of the order are under bond and no funds are paid out except upon approval of the proper official of each department of the work, the general funds of the order being subject to check only by the Imperial Treasurer and the Imperial Wizard.

No official of the organization is profiting from the funds received by the organization and all money coming from the various Klans and as a result of profit on regalia is being put into a reserve fund or property for the financial strengthening of the organization. Officials of the Ku Klux Klan are on salary and any member at any time can ascertain the exact amount of salaries paid. They are all reasonable and in most instances, in amounts considerably less than the same individuals could receive for the same work in commercial life.

The home given to Colonel William Joseph Simmons, the Imperial Wizard, was the gift of the individual members of the Knights of the Ku Klux Klan, the result of free-will offerings to the fund out of which it was purchased. Not a dollar of the funds of the order have gone into the cost of the home. As a matter of fact the committee in charge of the gift still has some funds to raise to complete the payment. Most of the gifts to this fund were under $5.

The organization quite recently has made two investments, one of which was deemed absolutely essential to keep pace with the tremendous growth of the order and to handle its constantly increasing business, and the other a pronouncedly essential feature in its work of teaching and preaching real Americanism.

The first was the purchase of a commodious building lot on Peachtree Road in Atlanta, Ga., to be used as the Imperial Palace, or national headquarters of the Knights of the Ku Klux Klan. The other was the purchase of Lanier University in Atlanta.

Colonel Simmons was elected president of Lanier University with power to appoint a new Board of Trustees, representing all sections of the country. It has been conducted as a Baptist institution for several years but in the future will be non-denominational. It is co-educational and its doors are open to the sons and daughters of all American citizens who believe that real Americanism should be taught the youth of America. Students of Lanier University, regardless of what other courses they may take, are required to take a course on the Constitution of the United States and a course in Bible study.

DEGREE FEES

Membership in this order cannot be bought; it is given as a reward for service unselfishly rendered. If you really believe in the order, and will practice its principles, and conform to its regulations and usages and contribute the sum of $10 toward its propagation and can otherwise qualify, then membership is awarded you upon this service rendered and pledge of future fidelity to the institution. This is *not* a selfish, mercenary, commercialized proposition, but the direct opposite.

THE INVISIBLE EMPIRE
KNIGHTS OF THE KU KLUX KLAN
(Incorporated)

OBJECTS AND PURPOSES
ARTICLE II

Section 1. The objects of this Order shall be—a common brotherhood of strict regulations for the purpose of cultivating and promoting real patriotism toward our Civil Government; to practice an honorable clanishness toward each other; to exemplify a practical benevolence; to shield the sanctity of the home and the chastity of womanhood; to maintain white supremacy; to teach and faithfully inculcate a high spiritual philosophy through an exalted ritualism, and by a practical devotedness to conserve, protect and maintain the distinctive institutions, rights, privileges, principles and ideals of a pure Americanism.

Sec. 2. To create and maintain an institution by and through which the present and succeeding generations shall commemorate and memoralize the great sacrifice, chivalric service and patriotic achievements of our original Society—the Ku Klux Klan of the reconstruction period of American history.

Sec. 3. This Order is an institution of chivalry, humanity, justice, and patriotism; embodying in its genius and principles all that is chivalric in conduct, noble in sentiment, generous in manhood and patriotic in purpose; its peculiar objects being: *First*—To protect the weak, the innocent, and the defenseless, from the indignities, wrongs and outrages of the lawless, the violent and the brutal; to relieve the injured and oppressed; to succor the suffering and unfortunate, especially worthy widows and orphans. *Second*—To protect and defend the Constitution of the United States of America, and all laws passed in conformity thereto, and to protect the states and the people thereof from all invasion of their rights thereunder from any source whatsoever. *Third*—To aid and assist in the execution of all constitutional laws, and to preserve the honor and dignity of the state by opposing tyranny, in any and every degree attempted from any and every source whatsoever, by a fearless and faithful administration of justice; to promptly and properly meet every behest of Duty "without fear and without reproach."

IMPERIAL PROCLAMATION [1]

To All Nations, People, Tribes and Tongues, and to the Lovers of Law and Order, Peace and Justice, of the Whole Earth, Greeting:

I, and the citizens of the Invisible Empire through me, proclaim to you as follows,—

We, the members of this Order desiring to promote real patriotism toward our Civil Government; honorable peace among men and nations; protection for and happiness in the homes of our people; love, real brotherhood, mirth and manhood among ourselves, and liberty, justice and fraternity among all mankind; and believing we can best accomplish these noble purposes through the channel of a high class mystic, social, patriotic, benevolent association, having a perfected lodge system, with an

[1] From A B C of the Ku Klux Klan. Ku Klux Klan Press, Atlanta, Georgia.

exalted ritualistic form of work and an effective form of government, not for selfish profit but for the mutual betterment, benefit and protection of all our oath-bound associates, their welfare physically, socially, morally and vocationally and their loved ones; do

PROCLAIM TO THE WHOLE WORLD

that we are dedicated to the sublime and pleasant duty of providing generous aid, tender sympathy and fraternal assistance in the effulgence of the light of life and amid the sable shadows of death; amid fortune and misfortune, and to the exalted privilege of demonstrating the practical utility of the great, yet most neglected, doctrine of the Fatherhood of God and the Brotherhood of Man as a vital force in the lives and affairs of men.

In this we invite all men who can qualify to become citizens of the Invisible Empire to approach the portal of our beneficent domain and join us in our noble work of extending its boundaries; in disseminating the gospel of "Klankraft," thereby encouraging, conserving, protecting and making vital the fraternal human relationship in the practice of a wholesome clanishness; to share with us the glory of performing the sacred duty of protecting womanhood; to maintain forever white supremacy in all things; to commemorate the holy and chivalric achievements of our fathers; to safeguard the sacred rights, exalted privileges and distinctive institutions of our Civil Government; to bless mankind, and to keep eternally ablaze the sacred fire of a fervent devotion to a pure Americanism.

The Invisible Empire is founded on sterling character, and immutable principles based upon a most sacred sentiment and cemented by noble purposes; it is promoted by a sincere, unselfish devotion of the souls of manly men and is managed and governed by the consecrated intelligence of thoughtful brains. It is the soul of chivalry and virtue's impenetrable shield; the devout impulse of an unconquered race.

Done in the Aulic of His Majesty, the Imperial Wizard and Emperor of the Invisible Empire, Knights of the Ku Klux Klan, in the Imperial Palace, in the Imperial City of Atlanta, Commonwealth of Georgia, United States of America, this the fourth day of July, Anno Domini Nineteen Hundred and Sixteen, Anno Klan L.

Signed by His Majesty,
William Joseph Simmons
Imperial Wizard.

DECLARATION [1]

WE SOLEMNLY DECLARE TO ALL MANKIND that the Knights of the Ku Klux Klan, incorporated, is the original, genuine Ku Klux Klan organized in the year 1866, and active

[1] Taken from the Constitution of the Order officially adopted September 29, 1916.

during the Reconstruction period of American history; and by and under its new corporate name is revived, reconstructed, remodeled, refined and expanded into a fraternal, patriotic, ritualistic society of national scope, duly incorporated under the laws of the State of Georgia, in the years 1915 and 1916, for the same spiritual purposes as it originally had and more particularly as set forth in Article II, of the Constitution and Laws of the Society.

WE DO FURTHER DECLARE TO THE WORLD that our original Prescript used as the governing law of the Ku Klux Klan, during the period of its former activities, and all official titles, mannerisms, usages and things therein prescribed have not been abandoned by us; but to the contrary all of such together with designs of paraphernalia, regalia, flags, banners, emblems, symbols or other insignia and things prescribed or previously used by or under the authority of the Ku Klux Klan are held sacred by us as a precious heritage; this precious heritage we shall jealously keep, forever maintain and valiantly protect from profanation. All of which are the property of the Ku Klux Klan under and by virtue of its now corporate name of Knights of Ku Klux Klan.

KU KLUX KREED [1]

WE, THE ORDER of the Knights of the Ku Klux Klan, reverentially acknowledge the majesty and supremacy of the Divine Being, and recognize the goodness and providence of the same.

WE RECOGNIZE our relation to the Government of the United States of America, the Supremacy of its Constitution, the Union of States thereunder, and the Constitutional Laws thereof, and we shall be ever devoted to the sublime principles of a pure Americanism and valiant in the defense of its ideals and institutions.

WE AVOW THE distinction between the races of mankind as same has been decreed by the Creator, and shall ever be true in the faithful maintenance of White Supremacy and will strenuously oppose any compromise thereof in any and all things.

WE APPRECIATE the intrinsic value of a real practical fraternal relationship among men of kindred thought, purpose and ideals and the infinite benefits accruable therefrom, and shall faithfully devote ourselves to the practice of an honorable Clanishness that the life and living of each may be a constant blessing to others.

[1] Original Creed Revised. Ku Klux Klan Press, Atlanta, Georgia.

WOMAN'S KLAN CREATED BY SIMMONS [1]

Declaring himself to be the founder, creator and supreme head of the Knights of the Ku Klux Klan and that he has at no time surrendered or partially surrendered the reigns of government of the Invisible Empire, Colonel William Joseph Simmons, Emperor of the Invisible Empire for life, broke his silence of more than two years with a proclamation declaring the existence of the woman's division of the Ku Klux Klan.

Designating himself as "El Magus" and naming the woman's division of the Klan the "Kamelia," Colonel Simmons officially sets at rest the persistent rumors that he is no longer in control of the Klan and verifies the current rumors regarding the formation of the woman's organization.

The proclamation in part says:

It was given to me, in the providence of Almighty God, with all of the limitations and restrictions of my humanity, to create by vision and to found in fact the Order of the Knights of the Ku Klux Klan. I have invested in the organization all that I have and all that I am so completely that nothing has been reserved. My life has been built into this great American institution. Therefore there are certain rights of supervision and regulation and control residing and inhering in me, as the creator and founder of the organization, which I shall continue to exercise as long as mortal life shall last.

In the course of human events the time has now come when the foundation shall be laid for the consummation of the other part of my early vision.

Always in my dream of a great renewal of Americanism and the reclamation of all that we have lost by alien and enemy invasion, there was the contemplation of a great woman's organization, adhering to the same principles, committed to the same purposes and impelled by the same motives as to organization as the Knights of the Ku Klux Klan. For a considerable period the demand upon me for an organization of women has increased until the demand has become a clamor from well-nigh every section of the United States.

A response to the appeal of the earnest, devoted, patriotic women of America cannot be longer deferred. They must take their place alongside the Knights of the Ku Klux Klan

[1] New York Journal. March 23, 1923.

and cooperate with them in all of their worthy movements and coordinate their activities with all of their noble enterprises, helping to save the white man's civilization on the American continent and thereby saving the white man's civilization throughout the world.

It is my peculiar privilege and honor and one of the proudest moments of my life, now and here to proclaim the creation and the foundation of the woman's organization to be known as Kamelia, and in making this proclamation, to declare as the founder and creator of the Kamelia my official designation and title to be "El Magus."

KU KLUX KLAN IN AMERICA [1]

The widespread belief that the purpose and policy of the Klan is violently to take the law in its own hands and run the country is not well founded. There have been instances of Klan violence in isolated sections, and Klansmen undoubtedly participated in an unusually revolting murder recently in Louisiana, but there is no reason to think that these things would not have occurred had there been no Klan. It is also true that in some states—particularly Georgia, Texas and Arkansas—a number of state officials have joined the Klan, and it is also true that in these states the politicians are seizing the opportunity which secret membership gives them to array on their side the religiously prejudiced voters. But it is also true that the business men who are running the organization are actively and earnestly interested in keeping its skirts free of lawlessness. Obviously, it is to their selfish interest to do so. Ultimately the kind of policy attributed to the Klan by the more violent of the newspapers would involve it with the federal government in such a way as to break it up.

The fact is, the meetings of the Klan are of a deeply religious and patriotic character, and the rank and file of its membership is made up of narrow-minded but well-meaning men, who believe they are helping to "save

[1] From article by Frank R. Kent, Vice-President of the Baltimore Sun. Spectator. 130 : 279-80. February 17, 1923.

the country." There is, in the vast bulk of them, no more possibility of violence than there would be in so many rabbits. Mostly, they are members of the same evangelical churches that support the Anti-Saloon League, and the Klan ritual, the fiery cross, the mask and the gown, the solemnity and secrecy of their gatherings, give them a veritable glow of self-righteousness, a smug feeling of rectitude, a cheap and entirely safe thrill. The wearing of the mask at the meetings is a part of the Simmons ritualistic tomfoolery, and its only sinister feature is the opportunity it affords ruffians in rural districts to use the Klan as a cloak and commit outrages in its name.

If there were space, I would like more deeply to analyse the psychology of the average Klan member and show exactly how the Kleagle baits the hook for him. All that can be done in this article, however, is to give certain conclusions, based on a somewhat thorough investigation, of the Klan situation made in a number of southern states where it is strongest. They are these: First, the men who run the Klan in Atlanta are an exceedingly "hard boiled" set of fellows who have placed it on a well-camouflaged but wholly commercial basis and are making a great deal of money out of it. They operate a non-sentimental selling organization and sell the Klan to "prospects" just as they would sell safety razors, insurance policies, garters or any other article. Second, the membership of the Klan is composed largely of well-meaning persons, who feel very much more deeply than they think, who have no sense of humour, but who are neither vicious nor dangerous. Third, the danger of the thing lies not so much in the Klan itself as in the screen it affords to politicians to profit through the religious issue and the temptation it offers to rough elements outside, and sometimes inside, to use the mask in violent outbreaks. Fourth, if the newspapers would cease daily denouncing the Klan, and if the Catholics and Jews were less excited and apprehensive concerning it, the organization would break of its own weight, because it is unsound at the bottom and uninformed and ignorant at the top.

SOME IDEALS OF THE KU KLUX KLAN [1]

1. THE CHARACTER OF THE ORGANIZATION

And here it is necessary to repeat briefly some things with which you are already familiar.

1. *This is a white man's organization,* exalting the Caucasian race and teaching the doctrine of white supremacy. This does not mean that we are enemies of the colored and mongrel races. But it does mean that we are organized to establish the solidarity and to realize the mission of the white race. All of Christian civilization depends upon the preservation and upbuilding of the white race, and it is the mission of the Ku Klux Klan to proclaim this doctrine until the white race shall come into its own.

2. *This is a gentile organization,* and as such has as its mission the interpretation of the highest ideals of the white, Gentile peoples. We sing no hymns of hate against the Jew. He is interested in his own things and we are exercising the same privilege of banding our own kind together in order that we may realize the highest and best possible for ourselves.

3. *It is an American organization,* and we do restrict membership to native-born American citizens. The records show that recently, at least, the aliens who have been flooding our land have come into this country, not because of any love for America, but, because of intolerable or unfavorable conditions in the land they left behind. They come to this country, not that they may contribute in any way to its growth and development, but that they may find opportunity to advance themselves and

[1] By William James Mahoney, Imperial Klokard, Knights of the Ku Klux Klan.

to serve their own interests. They are here to serve the interests of the land from which they came, regardless of the interests of this land in which they make their homes and seek their fortunes. They come to obey the mandates of governments of which they are still the subjects, even to the extent of endeavoring to break down the government under which they find protection while seeking their nefarious ends. In their hearts there is the tie that still binds them to the home-land; to them it is still the fatherland. Their sympathies are still there; their thoughts have been shaped by the currents in the old country. They do not easily re-adjust themselves. Thus we find the groups: Irish-Americans, German-Americans, and all kinds of hyphenated Americans. What pleasure would they find or what service could they render in this organization which is distinctively an American-American organization? We have organized to engender a real spirit of true Americanism—that Americanism which is a system based on a principle of utter antagonism to monarchism, whether represented by emperor, king, potentate, or pope.

4. *It is a Protestant organization.* Membership is restricted to those who accept the tenents of true Christianity, which is essentially Protestant. We maintain and contend that it is the inalienable right of Protestants to have their own distinctive organization. We can say to the world without apology, and say truly, that our forefathers founded this as a Protestant country and that it is our purpose to re-establish and maintain it as such. While we will energetically maintain and proclaim the principles of Protestantism, we will also maintain the principles of religious liberty as essential to the life and progress of this nation, and we will vigorously oppose all efforts to rob the American people of this right.

II. Racial Ideals

1. *We stand for white supremacy.* Distinction among the races is not accidental but designed. This is clearly

brought out in the one book that tells authoritatively of the origin of the races. This distinction is not incidental, but is of the vastest import and indicates the wisdom of the divine mind. It is not temporary but is as abiding as the ages that have not yet ceased to roll. The supremacy of the white race must be maintained, or be overwhelmed by the rising tide of color.

2. *We must keep this a white man's country.* Only by doing this can we be faithful to the foundations laid by our forefathers.

 a. This republic was established by white men.

 b. It was established for white men.

 c. Our forefathers never intended that it should fall into the hands of an inferior race.

 d. Every effort to wrest from white men the management of its affairs in order to transfer it to the control of blacks or any other color, or to permit them to share in its control, is an invasion of our sacred constitutional prerogatives and a violation of divinely established laws. Every effort to wrest from the white man the control of this country must be resisted. No person of the white race can submit to such efforts without shame. One of the sad facts in American political life is the readiness of so many politicians to sell their noble white birthright for a mess of black pottage. They would betray their race in order to win a few black votes.

 e. We would not rob the colored population of their right, but we demand that they respect the rights of the white race in whose country they are permitted to reside. When it comes to the point that they cannot and will not recognize and respect those rights, they must be reminded that this is a white man's country, so that they will seek for themselves a country more agreeable to their tastes and aspirations.

 f. Purity of the white blood must be maintained. One of the crying evils of the times is the mixture of white blood with that of negro. This evil has gone on since Colonial days until perhaps more than half of the negroes in the United States have some degree of white blood flowing in their veins. This condition is not only biologically disastrous but is giving rise to grave social problems. Mulatto leaders who, under present social conditions, are forced to remain members of the negro group and who aspire to white association because of their white blood are boldly preaching racial equality in all of its phases. The guilt for this state of affairs rests upon those members of the white race who have betrayed their own kind and bartered their own blood. It has become necessary to devise some means for the preservation of the white blood in its purity, because, despite prohibitive laws, racial inter-mixture is continuing and the problem of mixed blood is becoming more and more acute.

III. Citizenship Ideals

1. Development of the highest standard of citizenship. We ourselves must come to know what it means to be citizens of the foremost nation in all the earth. We need to have knowledge of the privileges and responsibilities and glories of our citizenship. And we need to be under the necessity of exercising our citizenship intelligently. We must learn and practice these things in order that we may teach them to others.

2. Rightful use of the ballot. Thank God, the day of partisan politics is past! Time was when parties stood for great principles. But today the difference between them is that of "tweedledum and tweedledee." One of the parties must be induced to champion great fundamental American principles that will hasten the development of our country, or else a new party must come into being. As the matter now stands we must cast our ballots for the right as it is most nearly represented and championed by men regardless of party.

3. We stand for the enforcement of law by the regularly constituted authorities. This order does not take

the law into its own hands and will not tolerate acts of lawlessness on the part of its members. Any man of any color or creed who charges the Ku Klux Klan with being an organization which fosters and perpetrates acts of lawlessness and deeds of violence is either wilfully blind or is a malicious, slandering, lying fool who, because of some inborn prejudice, seeks to destroy an organization that is law-abiding, and that demands the enforcement of laws by those who have been duly elected to office. We are within our rights as American citizens when we demand of men who are put in offices of trust that they shall faithfully perform the duties of their offices. It is quite evident that those who oppose us on this principle do not want the laws of our country enforced, and are seeking to cover their anarchistic spirit by impugning our motives and imputing criminality to us.

IV. Patriotic Ideals

The men of this order stand for the purest and most practical type of patriotism toward our great and glorious country.

1. We take our stand upon the Declaration of Independence as the basis of popular government. This document denies the dogma of despots, that kings rule by divine right. It asserts that governments derive their just powers from the consent of the governed. It solemnly affirms the right of the American people to govern themselves as a free and independent nation—independent of all outside sovereignty and control.

2. We believe in upholding the Constitution of the United States. This document reduces to practice the precepts of the Declaration and must be recognized as the supreme law of the land. It guarantees that liberty which must be cherished as the precious heritage of the American people. It establishes the freedom of institutions dear to the American heart. It guarantees religious

liberty, freedom of speech and of press, and all the rights that pertain to the people who constitute this nation. It depicts ideals and defines institutions that must be made real and kept secure. The Knights of the Ku Klux Klan are sworn by a solemn oath to uphold and defend this immortal Constitution.

3. Allegiance. We teach that the citizen's first and highest allegiance is to the government of the United States. No other government, potentate, or person of any kind shall share in this allegiance. We maintain that a divided allegiance means no allegiance. There can be no half American, and any sort of hyphen absolutely makes impossible any kind of loyalty to the American government, its ideals and institutions.

4. We stand for the American flag against enemies without and within. We emphasize devotion to the flag of our country as the ensign of our American Nationality and the emblem of our national honor. A man stands wholly for the Stars and Stripes or else to him his country's flag is only a dirty rag. We insist that no flag shall fly above our flag, and that no flag shall float by its side.

5. Neither domestic traitors nor foreign foes of any kind shall be permitted to destroy this nation.

6. None shall be allowed to circumscribe the influence and hinder the progress of American institutions on this continent. And this involves the welfare and development of the public school system. To those who seek to undermine or destroy this American institution we say, "hands off," and we will defend this institution against every enemy, whether it be political or ecclesiastical.

V. Christian Ideals

1. We magnify the Bible—as the basis of our Constitution, the foundation of our government, the source of our laws, the sheet-anchor of our liberties, the most practical guide of right living, and the source of all true wisdom.

2. We teach the worship of God. For we have in mind the divine command, "Thou shalt worship the Lord thy God."

3. We honor the Christ, as the Klansman's only *criterion of character*. And we seek at His hands that cleansing from sin and impurity, which only He can give.

4. We believe that the highest expression of life is in service and in sacrifice for that which is right; that selfishness can have no place in a true Klansman's life and character; but that he must be moved by unselfish motives, such as characterized our Lord the Christ and moved Him to the highest service and the supreme sacrifice for that which was right.

I have but suggested here a few of the many ideals of the Ku Klux Klan. Let us seek to make these real in our life and practice so that we may become bright, true Klansmen, and be ready for other ideals and principles as they shall be presented from time to time.

VIEW OF KLAN FROM INSIDE[1]

View of Klan from inside presented below by Edward Young Clarke, Grand Wizard pro tem:

With at least 80 per cent of the newspapers of the country bitterly attacking the Knights of the Ku Klux Klan upon every conceivable angle, augmented by the desperate efforts of misguided philanthropists, political charioteers, and certain religious and racial groups who have nothing in common with Anglo-Saxon ideals, this purely American order is not only holding its own, but enjoying phenomenal growth.

Arguments against the Klan are invariably based upon false premises. For instance, there is the oft-repeated charge that this organization metes out justice from its own tribunals, an allegation that has never been proven. Another accusation, popular with the anti-Klan forces, is that the sole purpose of the order is to feed the fires of racial and religious hatred. Again, the public is led to believe that this institution is made up of fanatics, degenerates, brigands, and every sort of enemy to society. We are socialists or anti-socialists, reformers or law-breakers, "wet" or "dry," religious or sacriligious, depending upon the personal sentiments of our accuser.

[1] Literary Digest. 74 : 51-2. August 5, 1922.

We are denounced because, by right of our sacred inheritance, we glory in wearing the regalia of the original Ku Klux Klan as a memorial to that dauntless organization of the reconstruction days. The unthinking public condemns us for our strategy in fighting secrecy with secrecy. They censure us because we are sworn to safeguard the welfare and the noble blood of the Caucasian race, to preserve the traditions of the Republic, to propagate our Christian faith! And it is surely significant that the most violent opposition emanates from racial and religious groups who have nothing in common with those principles.

The Knights of the Ku Klux Klan do not expect to have their principles and working policies universally approved. Every cause has its worthiness questioned. Every issue has its proponents and opponents. But every movement that claims a worthy motive is certainly entitled to fair play, and the Knights of the Ku Klux Klan are no exception.

Opposition to this organization is mainly psychological. It is made up of senseless inhibitions and the associations of ideas. No person has yet presented a logical reason as to why a secret organization sworn to uphold the law, to propagate Christianity, and to perpetuate American ideals, should not exist. I say that no person has done this, unless, of course, he ignores the most vital urges known to man—self-preservation and the safeguarding of the home.

The Knights of the Ku Klux Klan owe their tremendous growth, not to the efforts of professional organizers, but to its individual members. Those who have crossed the portals of the Invisible Empire have found there a great human machine, whose ideals are an inspiration to any God-fearing Christian, and whose ranks are peopled with sane, intelligent and honest men.

The modern Klan is not, as our enemies charge, a revival of Knownothingism. It is not a political party, it will take no part in political controversies, and it has nothing to do with partizan issues. Klansmen will follow the dictates of their individual conscience in casting their votes. As an organization, we have no candidates—no favored party.

This organization came into existence as an honest attempt to solve certain well-defined problems concerning the interest of those whose forefathers established the nation. It is this force of things, this necessity for national solidarity which has brought the Klan into being.

DEFENSE OF THE KU KLUX KLAN [1]

This editor (of Shuler's Magazine) has repeatedly affirmed privately and publicly that he is not a member

[1] Literary Digest. 76 : 18-19. January 20, 1923.

of the Ku Klux or any other secret organization. But when it comes to secret societies, he sees no difference absolutely between the Ku Klux and many others, the Knights of Columbus, for instance. The Knights of Columbus has an oath, just as binding, or more so, than the Ku Klux oath. Moreover, the Knights of Columbus' oath is not one-half so American as is the Ku Klux. If you charge that the Ku Klux has put over mobs, I answer that the Knights of Columbus has put over two mobs to where any other secret organization on earth has ever put over one.

This editor has been favored recently by being permitted to look over documentary evidence as to the tenets, principles and aims of the Ku Klux Klan. He finds that this organization stands with positive emphasis for Americanism as opposed to foreign idealism; for the principles of the Christian religion as opposed to Roman Catholicism and infidelity; for the American public schools and for the placing of the Holy Bible in the schoolrooms of this nation; for the enforcement of the laws upon the statute books and for a wholesome respect for the Constitution of the United States; for the maintenance of virtue among American women, sobriety and honor among American men, and for the eradication of all agencies and influences that would threaten the character of our children. So the principles of the Klan are not so damnable as pictured, it would seem.

This organization is opposing the most cunning, deceitful and persistent enemy that Americanism and Protestant Christianity have ever had—the Jesuits. Speaking of "invisible empires," of forces that creep through the night and do their dirty work under cover, influences that are set going in the secret places of darkness, the Jesuits are the finished product. They have burned, killed, defamed, blackmailed, and ruined their enemies by the hundreds. History reeks with it. Tho I disagree with the logic of the Klan, the members of that organization declare that they can only fight such a foe by using his own fire.

As to the charge that the Ku Klux Klan has functioned in mob violence in their efforts to correct conditions, I have this to say: I am convinced that most of the mobs reported have not been ordered and directed by the Klan as an organization. I am moreover convinced that many of them have been put over by forces opposed to the Klan and for the purpose of seeking to place the guilt for mob rule upon the Klan. The most of these mobs have been, according to investigation, not Ku Klux mobs at all, but gatherings of indignant citizens, bent on correcting conditions that the officers of the law refused to correct. The way to cause the Ku Klux to retire from the field is for the officers of the law to take that field and occupy it.

The Ku Klux has the same right to exist so long as it obeys the law that any other organization has. We have not heard of any investigation of the Knights of Columbus, altho the un-American oaths are historic and their mob activities have been repeatedly published and heralded from platforms far and near.

LAW-ABIDING ORDER [1]

The Imperial Wizard in a full-page advertisement in the New York Herald says:

There is nothing in the Constitution of the order that any honorable, law-abiding, conscientious, clean-hearted, and pure-spirited, 100 per cent American could not swear to and uphold. The Knights of the Ku Klux Klan does not encourage or foster lawlessness, racial prejudice, or religious intolerance and is not designed to act in the capacity of a law-enforcement or moral-correction agency except in so far as the members of the organization as citizens may be able to assist the regular officers of the law in the apprehending of criminals and the upholding and sustaining of the majesty of the law and the honor and integrity of the Stars and Stripes and the Constitution of the United

[1] Literary Digest. August 27, 1921.

States of America. To the above every member entering the portals of this organization has been sworn under the most binding and solemn oath, and any act or word contrary to the above statement by any Klansman is a violation of his oath and puts him beyond the pale of fellowship in the organization and makes him an outlaw not only in the eyes of the law of the land, but in the eyes of his former fellow Klansmen, as a violation of oath of any Klansman automatically banishes him from this organization.

I hereby declare and pronounce the present attempt to fasten upon this organization acts of lawlessness to be the attempt of our enemies to discredit the organization, and the further our investigation goes into every particular incident of lawlessness which has been charged against us the more convinced I am that the present wave of criticism passing through the press is a concerted move on the part of our enemies in an attempt to prejudice the public in regard to our work.

In conclusion, the Knights of the Ku Klux Klan is a law-abiding, legally chartered, standard fraternal order, designed to teach and inculcate the purest ideals of American citizenship, with malice toward none and justice to every citizen regardless of race, color, or creed.

FOES OF KU KLUX[1]

Who are the enemies of the Klan? First of all, there is the Roman Catholic church, against which we have directed no attack and upon which we now make no war. The Roman Catholic church has a right to found and maintain itself for the promulgation of its distinctive religious tenets on American soil, and so long as that institution confines itself to activities that belong distinctively to a religious organization its rights under the American flag, guaranteed by the Constitution, can never be invaded or even questioned.

But when the Roman Catholic church interferes with our fundamental principle of separation of church and state, when it interferes with rights guaranteed in the Constitution of free speech and the right of peaceable assembly, when it undertakes to usurp any of the powers or functions of government, when it undertakes in any

[1] From address of H. W. Evans, Imperial Wizard of Dallas, Texas. New York Times. December 7, 1922.

wise to make the United States of America a province of Rome, then the institution has challenged the white, native-born Protestant Christian of America to defend this republic against invasion or else surrender the republic to the domination of the foreign ecclesiastical potentate.

He asserted that the Jewish race was allied with the Catholics in successive assaults on the Klan "because the Jew in America sees in the rise and extension of Klanishness an arrest placed upon his activities in money getting.

The Jew produces nothing anywhere on the face of the earth. He does not till the soil. He does not create or manufacture anything for common use. He adds nothing to the sum of human welfare. Everywhere he stands between the producer and the consumer and sweats the toil of the one and the necessity of the other for his gains.

THE KU KLUX KLAN LAW [1]

There is a federal law against Ku Klux Klanism. It was passed in 1871 after Congress had investigated the white riders and their activities. This law calls night-riding "rebellion." It makes it a "high crime" to "go upon the highways or upon the premises of another with the intent to deprive any person of the protection of the law; to hinder state authorities from providing such protection of the law; to impede the course of justice in any manner."

President Grant was, and other presidents likewise are, authorized by this law to employ the army and navy, if necessary, to restore order in any state where "rebellion" exists, if the local authorities fail to protect citizens from offenses of marauders. The president may suspend

[1] By William G. Shepherd. Leslie's Illustrated Weekly Magazine. 133 : 346 September 10, 1921.

the writ of habeas corpus in any state where local officials cannot preserve the peace against "rebellion." No person may act as a juror in a case against a member of the forbidden "combination or conspiracy" who cannot swear that he has not been a member of the organization. All cases, under the law, are to be tried in federal courts. Any person who has knowledge that an offense is committed, and does not notify the authorities, can be fined $5,000, the money to go to the widow, or next-of-kin, of the person losing his life in "such outrage."

The penalty for Ku Klux Klanism, though the law does not specifically mention the Ku Klux Klan, is a fine of from $500 to $5,000; imprisonment, with or without hard labor, for six months to six years. Injured persons may also collect damages from the guilty parties.

INVISIBLE GOVERNMENT [1]

If there is one thing more than another that Americans require of their political affairs, it is that they should be open, aboveboard, and discussable by all. Invisible government and secret influences form the antithesis to democracy. We have and will maintain freedom of speech and of the press, subject only to the apothegm stated the other day in these columns, "Personal liberty ends where public injury begins."

The most moderate program put forth by defenders of the revived Ku Klux Klan shows its purpose to influence legislation, public opinion, and political elections. It has a right to do all this if it acts openly and fairly. It has no right to work secretly by underground methods to inflame racial and religious prejudice in order to bring about political or legislative action. If one says this to a defender of the Klan, he replies, "Well, the Knights of Columbus do the same thing." We have seen no evidence

[1] Outlook. 132 : 643. December 13, 1922.

of this; but, if it is so, then that or any other organization so acting is subject to precisely the same criticism. Meanwhile it is notorious and self-evident that the Klan cunningly tries to twist into one cord the three hateful strands of anti-Jewish, anti-Catholic, and anti-negro prejudice. Help yourself, in effect the Klan says, to your own special hatred! All this is distinctly un-American.

There is no objection to secret societies in themselves. Any one can name off-hand several that are admirable as sources of social enjoyment, of mutual benefit, of fraternal benevolence. Ceremony and ritual are attractive to many people, and it is true that many secret societies are not merely harmless, but beneficial. Yet, in order that the worthy associations should not be confounded with the objectionable, it is at least desirable that all should be registered with the state authorities and the names of their responsible officers be available for purposes of inquiry. Emphatically this is desirable in the case of an organization like the Ku Klux Klan, founded originally as an instrument of terrorism, and lately revived in an effort to foster race and religious animosity and to throw the influence of its secretly banded members on this or that side of a political issue. We are not permitted to know when and why the Klan's influence is thus exerted, and in such a situation fair discussion is impossible. Just lately, for instance, one newspaper correspondent remarked:

> One of the surprises of this year's election was the success of a candidate for Governor of Oregon, with Ku Klux support, and the adoption by the voters of that state of a law designed to do away with *all private* schools and all parochial schools at which a feature of the teaching is instruction in religious matters.

It may be that the Ku Klux Klan was influential in the election of a governor in Oregon and in the adoption of the school law—and it may not; how can we tell what an oath-bound society has done? The same thing applies to the election of Senator Mayfield in Texas, "said to be" due to Klan efforts. We don't want "said to be" in

American political life, we want open politics as well as open diplomacy.

NATION-WIDE FIGHT ON KLAN [1]

The Klan will be wrecked by the exposure of its personnel, Mr. Rutledge of the American Unity League said at the Hotel McAlpin last evening.

We intend to publish the names of the New York City Klansmen, for our experience in Chicago has demonstrated to us that the sure way to kill the Klan is by publishing the names of the individual members.

This is so, because the individual Klansman fears public sentiment, and as soon as he becomes known as a Klansman he resigns or ceases his activities. So far we have not only had no libel action against us in Chicago for the publication of a name wrongfully, but there has not been one case in which it was established that we had published a name through error.

Scores of Klansmen are coming to our Chicago offices every day to ask what they can do to keep their names from being published. We have told each of these men to send in his resignation and get it accepted by the King Kleagle of the Realm of Illinois, and his name would not be published. A great many resignations from the Klan have come about in this way.

When we began the publication of the names of Klansmen in Chicago, the Klan, according to our information, had a membership of about fifty-five thousand. Now it has dropped to about ten thousand. The Unity League was established about seven months ago and started the publication of the names after three months of preliminary work.

The publication of the names of Klansmen will be only part of the work to be done by the league throughout the country. The league will approach Congress and

[1] New York Times. December 7, 1922.

the Legislatures of states in which it is organized and ask for the enactment of laws against masked organizations.

No member of the Ku Klux Klan can hold office in the United States without being guilty of treason. The oath of allegiance that the Ku Kluxer takes to his "Emperor" makes it impossible for him to be true to the government of the United States.

Our entire program being one of education and the creation of better feeling between the several racial and religious groups making up America, we do not fight the Klansman with his own weapons, social, commercial and political boycott, but we do make it unpopular to be affiliated with the Klan by showing members and prospects the dangerous activities of the organization.

WHY OF THE KU KLUX [1]

Sir: Suppress the Ku Klux? By all means, but while we are suppressing it we need to discover the cause. Are there reasons for the rise of such movements? Is the Ku Klux the outward manifestation of an inner poison and will the body politic be permanently cured only when the disease is healed?

There are many features of this evil, but two especially serious ones can be named. First, throughout all classes there is a growing scepticism of democracy, especially of the current American brand. Many Americans believe that there is little even-handed justice administered in the courts; that a poor man has little chance against a rich one; that many judges practically buy their places on the bench or are put there by powerful interests. The strong, able young man comes out of college ready to do his part in politics, but with the settled conviction that unless he can give full time there is no use "bucking

[1] By Mary W. Herring, New Republic. 33 : 289. February 7, 1923.

up against the machine." Furthermore he believes the machines to be equally corrupt. "The miner in West Virginia sees the power of the state enlisted on the side of the mine owner. The citizens of New York, Chicago and Boston are under the bondage of corrupt machines working through Hylan, Thompson and Curley. The young officer sent to Washington for office duty during the war came back with the belief that graft prevailed everywhere. Men are asking whether perhaps after all autocracy is not better than democracy. They feel helpless to meet existing conditions. Many would like to be good citizens but do not know how to make any headway against the machine.

There is an ominous lack of good leadership. Most men of ability and character are unwilling to make the necessary sacrifices required in accepting office. In consequence the inferior or the corrupt often take the places left vacant through the others' evasion of duty.

When law breaks down, lynch law takes its place. The tyranny of the corrupt politician is replaced by the tyranny of mob rule. A mob has many parts: it may have a nucleus of honest-minded people, who genuinely believe that only in this way can justice be attained. The Fascisti in Italy and the Ku Klux in this country have much in common—loyalty to the best interests of the country is loudly proclaimed, while their aims are promoted by violence and tyranny. Training in the ranks of the better elements are the suspicious and the violent— the haters and the mischief-makers. Ignorance is always an easy victim of fear and suspicion, and such a movement among the unintelligent may start a blaze not easily put out.

We may cease to fear movements of this kind only when America becomes a law-abiding country; when our courts are above suspicion; when the rights of free speech and opinion are restored, when the rich and the poor become equal before the courts—when our governments in nation, state, city and town become honest. If we will not take the laborious path of faithful citizenship —if good and able men and women will not consent to lead us, then once in so often these short cuts to justice will be taken.

A second element of this national disease is the presence of large organizations which under the sanction of religion are permitted to gather great stores of money which are secretly collected and secretly disbursed. Every year new pressure is put upon business and politics to publish a report of all money handled. Newberry could have passed ten years ago more easily than he can today. Great business corporations are finding it increasingly difficult to keep their books from the questioning eyes of the public. The mine operators will soon have to reveal their gains to the world.

Secrecy always breeds suspicion. The fear and suspicion felt of the Roman Catholic and Mormon churches is based largely on their unwillingness to report receipts and expenditures. People have no disposition to control their beliefs; we are all too anxious to have freedom for ourselves, but they do object to such stores of treasure being held by strong organizations endowed with the added power of religious authority. How is this money used? Does it shape our public schools, determine the contents of the public libraries, elect senators, congressmen, and justices of the Supreme Court? Does it prevent the formation of a department of education at Washington? Does this money give the Mormon church the balance of power in a presidential election and control business which in turn affects the national welfare? No organization, religious or secular, should be permitted to close its books against state inspection. If it is doing nothing of which it need be ashamed it will not wish to do so. Religious and charitable institutions should be above suspicion. We believe that a "state cannot exist half slave and half free." Do we also realize that it cannot survive half democratic and half autocratic? If the Mormon and Roman Catholic churches wish to have peace and friendly relations with their neighbors, let them come out frankly and open their books. So long as this secrecy lasts suspicion and fear will last. So long as this suspicion and fear last there will be a festering sore in our body politic and such freakish and often criminal organizations as the Ku Klux will be the outer manifestation of this inner poison. Honest government and publicity in the handling of money are vital conditions of public health.

KU KLUX AN INDICTMENT OF LOCAL OFFICERS [1]

Judge Hamilton is exactly right. The rise of the Ku Klux Klan is the effort of citizens to secure redress for the refusal of officers to enforce the law and that, too, by direct action. Wherever the Ku Klux Klan operates it is a clear indication that some public officers, not necessarily all of them, have previously violated their oath of office in refusing to enforce the law.

Judge Hamilton goes on to say, "The Constitution of this state says the defendant has the right of trial by a jury of his peers under the supervision of the court." Here, again, Judge Hamilton is right. But, have not the citizens of the state an equal right to demand that the criminal shall be tried by a jury of his peers? We think so. But by the laws of Texas an officer can decide whether or not the criminal shall be punished or not, and the citizenship have no redress except through the Ku Klux Klan.

Judge Hamilton further says, "The fault lies with the officers. A public office is not a private snap, but a position of public trust, and any officer who is incom-

[1] Literary Digest. September 24, 1921.

petent or derelict of his duties or unwilling to attend to them with the same degree and caution as he would attend to his own private business is disqualified and unfit to hold an office of public trust, and it is the duty of this Grand Jury to make a careful investigation of the officers of this court and see that they are performing their duties as the law directs."

These words are well said by Judge Hamilton. The trouble lies with our law for the removal of officers. Except for the one crime of crooked financial dealing, no officer has ever been removed from office in Texas so far as can be revealed by thorough state-wide investigation. As the law stands today our peace officers can do as they please. They can say to one criminal—"Go ahead with your operations," or to another that he "must stop his criminal operations" and the state has no control over the officers. As the law stands today if the citizens want in a legal way to take action against such an officer, a private citizen must enter a civil suit on his own initiative, bear the complete expense himself and fight it through the courts with every obstacle imaginable placed in his way to defeat him. If the man is guilty of crooked financial dealing he can get action; otherwise the records fail to show that any successful action has ever resulted from the dereliction of officers in Texas.

The good citizens of Texas finding that they have no redress in the laws of our state have organized the Ku Klux Klan. We do not believe in the method of the Ku Klux Klan; we believe it is fraught with great danger, but we do not believe that the proper way to proceed is to bring down our vituperation upon the Ku Klux; better far that we correct the law and make it easy to remove a corrupt officer from office, and take such action as shall cause our public officials to no longer regard their office as a "public snap" but "rather a public trust," as Judge Hamilton says.

KU KLUX KLAN RADICALLY WRONG [1]

Gradually a feeling developed within me that there was something wrong with the organization—that it was not the sort of "fraternal society" to which I had been accustomed for nearly twenty years. I thought at first that this was due to the fact that I had done so much lodge work in my lifetime that I was growing stale. But, certain portions of the obligation, which at first had seemed merely perfunctory, stood out in my mind and challenged serious thought and consideration.

I studied everything I could find to help me in my work; I received printed matter from the organization; I talked with Klansmen from other cities; and I delved deeply into the origin and history of the original Ku Klux Klan. But business men of standing and prominence in the places where I worked asked me pointed questions about the organization, questions that I could not answer and on which I could get no satisfactory answers from above. Slowly my vague fears that there was something vitally wrong crystallized into stronger belief. I spoke to a few close friends in the organization and asked them to give me their frank opinions about it. Without any prompting from me they voiced the same thoughts and gave expression to the same doubts that I had myself.

After much thoughtful deliberation I reached the decision that the Ku Klux Klan obligation was radically wrong. It was not the kind of obligation men take in *fraternal* organizations—it was a *political* organization. I saw that the ritual, which had previously been to me merely a badly written mass of words, was really a sacriligious mockery. I realized that the whole scheme was vicious in principle and a menace to the peace and safety

[1] By Henry P. Fry. From his introduction in "The Modern Ku Klux Klan." Copyright. Small, Maynard and Company, Boston. 1922. Reprinted by permission.

of America. The basis for these conclusions can be stated briefly:

First. While the organization was incorporated under the laws of the state of Georgia as a fraternal order, the claim being advanced by the promoters that it should have similar powers to the Masons and Knights of Pythias, it is not a fraternal organization in the sense usually understood, but an attempt to create in this republic of ours an "Invisible Empire," entirely political and military in nature and designed to function bodily.

Second. The "Invisible Empire" is under the control of one man who openly calls himself an "Emperor," holds position for life, and exercises despotic control over the affairs of the organization.

Third. Candidates—designated as "aliens"—who are received into the organization, are not regarded as "members" but as "citizens" of this "Invisible Empire," and instead of being "initiated," as is usually the case in fraternal orders, are "naturalized" and become "subjects" of the "Emperor."

Fourth. Membership is restricted to a limited class of American citizens, including only white, Gentile, American-born Protestants; all other Americans being ineligible.

Fifth. In propagating this "Invisible Empire," the work, which is being done all over the United States by a highly paid and highly efficient field force, is being carried on by stirring up prejudice and hatred against the Catholic, the Jew, the negro and the foreign-born American citizen.

Sixth. Under the claim of the enforcement of "law and order," the "Invisible Empire" is attempting to take into its grasp the entire law-enforcing machinery of the United States, including the officers and the men of the regular army and reserve corps, the national guard, sheriffs and their deputies, mayors, police officials, men, judges and all persons connected with law administration, with the exception of those ineligible under the rules above stated.

Seventh. The "citizens" of the "Invisible Empire are urged by the organization to purchase white robes and helmets, which are used for the purpose of going abroad in disguise for the concealment of the identity of the wearer, and in many localities there have been parades and demonstrations of strength made by the organization, all having the effect of intimidating certain classes of people of these communities.

Eighth. The sale of these robes is a monopoly in the hands of the Gate City Manufacturing Company, a concern associated with the organization, and from this monopoly somebody is deriving an enormous revenue.

Ninth. The propagation of the organization is being conducted in such a way that it is clearly a money making scheme run for the benefit of a few insiders.

Tenth. The claim that this is the "genuine original Klan" is a historical fraud, not supported by the history and prescript of the old Klan which are available for public inspection.

Eleventh. The Ku Klux Klan propaganda is vicious, un-American and evil and will have a tendency to stir up racial and religious hatred in this country to such an extent as to result, unless checked, in a serious religious-racial war.

Twelfth. The ritualistic work, while clumsy, ignorant, plagiaristic, and poorly written is an attempt to use the cloak of religion to promote the financial fortunes of the insiders; and its principal feature—the ceremony of "naturalization"—is a mockery and parody on the sacred and holy rite of baptism.

Thirteenth. The organization should be exposed for what it is, and the Congress of the United States should enact suitable legislation to make it illegal and bar its literature and propaganda from the mails.

Fourteenth. Suitable and necessary legislation should

be enacted by Congress and the state legislatures of a general nature which will forever prevent the organization and operation of a secret movement of this character.

GREAT BIGOTRY MERGER [1]

The World's exposure so advertised the organization that although it lost many of the better members it added a large following of riff-raff, and the Klan is now capitalizing the failure of the Rules Committee of the House of Representatives to report on its investigation.

In twenty-seven states the Klan has made nearly two hundred public appearances in hoods in the last ten months. Most of these appearances have been at churches, charitable meetings, or rallies for the Salvation Army, the Red Cross, the Boy Scouts, etc. Invariably gifts of money or Bibles or flags have been made. Masked men have also turned up at numerous funerals, strewn flowers upon the coffin, and dispersed. All this is pure bidding for publicity. But it is significant that the gifts to churches and to charity have been most numerous where the Klan outrages have been most flagrant. Thus, in Texas eighty-seven visitations of Christian charity have been paraded before the people.

In Texas the Ku Klux Klan has become the instrument of a new negro enslavement, for it is employed in forcing black men to work and pick cotton at rates they would not accept if the decision were left to themselves. Throughout the south and southwest the negro population lives in constant fear of the hooded bands of nightriders. Everywhere, south, north, east, and west, where the Klan has planted the fiery cross of the Invisible Empire, Roman Catholics and Jews are the intended targets, while on the Pacific coast the Japanese are included among the objects of 100 per cent American vigilance.

[1] From article by Charles P. Sweeney. Nation. 115 : 8-10. July 5, 1922.

KU KLUX KLAN

The law may as well not exist. It is flouted and laughed at. In states where Klan organization has reached its highest point the administrators themselves are Klansmen. Murders, kidnappings, floggings, threats—they are almost daily occurrences. But a judge who denounces the night-riding mobs is the exception. A sheriff, Bob Buchanan, at Waco, Texas, with courage enough to stop a masked parade and demand the names of the paraders, is shot and then made a victim of removal proceedings sponsored by the most influential citizens of his county. A Klansman, in Birmingham, Alabama, who kills a Catholic priest in cold bood on his own doorstep is acquitted at the "trial" amidst the plaudits of the mob. A city council in the same "Birmingham the Beautiful," considering an ordinance forbidding masked parades on the public streets, is terrorized in its own chamber into defeating the measure. Members of a board of education in Atlanta, Georgia, demurring at voting for a resolution to dismiss all Catholics employed as public school teachers, receive letters threatening their lives. A mayor in Columbus, Georgia, who refuses to remove a city manager who has proved efficient and capable finds his home dynamited; the city manager, "a blue-bellied Yankee," is driven from the city. A Roman Catholic church, at Naperville, Illinois, is destroyed by an incendiary fire two hours after a monster Klan midnight initiation in the neighborhood.

From the south and southeast reports have come that the Klan is on both sides of the prohibition question. In one section Klansmen manifest a determination to drive out all bootleggers, as for instance in Wilson, Oklahoma, in January last, when Klansmen attempted to banish Joe Carrol, a reputed bootlegger, who pulled his gun and fired, killing two Klansmen, and then received a fatal bullet himself.

In Georgia, the Klan is generally regarded as the protecting arm of the bootlegger, the regulator of men who do not live with their wives, and the arch-enemy of Catholics in politics. In Texas the Klan is likewise very anti-Catholic, very moral, and very wet. In Texas and Colorado fearless judges have held that the Klan oath is an impediment to justice. Judge Robert Street at Beaumont, Texas, removed Tom Garner, sheriff of Jefferson County, on the ground that his Klan oath was in contravention of his oath of office. In Colorado it was held that witnesses who refused to answer questions because it would violate their Klan oath were in contempt of court, and three Klansmen were jailed; also when the Klan threatened death to Governor Shoup's negro messenger unless he left the state, and by threats did succeed in driving from the state another reputable negro citizen, the state authorities refused a charter to the order.

In their statements to the press, nevertheless, Simmons and Clarke continue to insist that the Klan is not governed by bigotry or prejudice and that it is not anti-Catholic. There is a volume of proof to refute this, but hardly more is needed than these excerpts from an address by Simmons, himself, to the Junior Order of United American Mechanics in Atlanta on April 30, last, as published in the Searchlight, organ of the Ku Klux Klan and the leading journalistic proponent of the Great American Fraternity:

> Right here within our own borders, the great and mighty city of Boston, which tries to lay claim that it is the cradle of America (tries is all it can do), and holds itself up as the paragon of American principles, has, if my information is correct, seventeen schools in which the English language is never spoken, and not an English thought or an American ideal. These schools are for the children of French-Canadians who have come across the border and each of these schools are under the domination of a foreign potentate who is in nowise sympathetic with American ideals and institutions. Right here in our own land twenty-one towns in the state of Connecticut are under the domination and control of the Italian-Dago influence. Then you hear folks talk about "we Americans," and of America as the melting-pot where the stamp and impress of all nations can come in and shape our destinies. It is no such thing. It is a garbage can! Not a melting-pot. . . My

friends, your government can be changed between the rising and the setting of one sun. This great nation, with all it provides, can be snatched away from you in the space of one day, and that day no more than ten hours. When the hordes of aliens walk to the ballot box and their votes outnumber yours, then that alien horde has got you by the throat. . . Americans will awake from their slumber and rush out for battle and there will be such stir as the world has never seen the like. The soil of America will run with the blood of its people.

In this same address the Colonel, who before Congress denied that he or the Klan held anti-negro prejudices, said:

All these folks of color can take their place—they had better take it and stay in it when they get in it. This is a white man's civilization and we are the instrumentalities for the preservation thereof and the protection of that which was created by years of devotion, which has given to the world the open Bible, the little red school house, if you please, the great public-school system, all those things which have come to us through years of devout thought and hard work as a sacred heritage. . . Men tell me that the negroes in this state, and I am not now going outside the state of Georgia, are paying their poll taxes for as far back as fourteen years and qualifying to vote. . . I am informed that every buck nigger in Atlanta who attains the age of twenty-one years has gotten the money to pay his poll tax and register, and that six thousand of them are now ready to vote, and that these apes are going to line up at the polls, mixed up there with white men and white women. Lord forgive me, but that is the most sickening and disgusting sight you ever saw. You've got to change that. . . Keep the negro and the other fellow where he belongs. They have got no part in our political or social life. If in one, he will get into the other.

These words of the Imperial Wizard of the Invisible Empire are mild, indeed conservative, when compared with the violence of Carl F. Hutcheson, Atlanta school commissioner, J. O. Wood, editor of the Searchlight, or Walter Sims, Atlanta city councilman and Klan candidate for mayor. The first two of these are the principal promoters of the Great American Fraternity, and Hutcheson's law partner, J. A. Morris, is president. With their confreres they actually induced the Klan to boycott a certain brand of cigarettes (Camels) because they are made by a concern reputed to be controlled by Thomas Fortune Ryan, a Catholic. They have attempted to intimidate the Atlanta Board of Education into dismissing all of the Roman Catholics employed as school teachers, to influence employers to dismiss their Roman Catholic workers, and to boycott merchants who display Roman Catholic sympathies. Wood, a Klan candidate for the legislature in Georgia, has chosen as a leading plank in his platform a more rigid inspection of convents and institutions conducted by religious orders. The Klan, several weeks ago, succeeded in effecting the dismissal of a school principal in El Paso, Texas, because she is a Catholic. This writer is in possession of first-hand information concerning a conference between several of these fanatics, in which Clarke, perceiving the salability of anti-Catholic activities, proposed the very plan now revealed under the title the Great American Fraternity. It is interesting to add that at a similar conference, sometime previous, Clarke worked up his hearers with a declaration that when the Klan influence flowered its leaders would aim at the sterilization of all male negro children so that the negro would gradually disappear from the American Continent. It is equally interesting that negroes are joining the Catholic church for self-protection.

Clarke denies he is back of the Great American Fraternity. Nevertheless the idea is his. And this is the idea:

1. To organize a nation-wide sales organization composed of members of thirteen secret orders popularly believed to be hostile to the Catholic church.

2. To instruct these salesmen in the business of selling effective political anti-Catholicism to their brothers in their respective lodges. This is in line with the system adopted by Clarke in 1920 for putting over the Ku Klux. At that time Clarke suddenly realized the value of representing the Klan to be "the fighting brother" of Masonry. So he issued orders that none but men with Masonic

KU KLUX KLAN

affiliations should be employed as Kleagles, or salesmen, although Clarke himself is not a Mason and it is well understood that he could not get into the order.

3. To find political issues, based on opposition to the Catholic church and to Catholics, upon which all of the thirteen secret societies might unite in a given city, county, or state.

This idea is now a realized fact. Hutcheson and Wood, law partners until recently, had the Great American Fraternity incorporated in Georgia and set the price of membership at $5, payable in advance upon application. The only other requirement is that the applicant produce evidence that he is a member in good standing of one or another of the thirteen organizations. The fact that the most prominent Masons of the country, as well as officials of the Orangemen, have repudiated the plot as anti-American does not worry the promoters. They are out to unite in a single group of haters all the haters in the country...

Already, and without the stimulating activity of the Great American Fraternity, Ku Klux hatred has forced its way to a greater or less degree into the politics of ten or more of the states. In Texas Robert L. Henry, twenty years a member of Congress, now a candidate for Culberson's seat in the Senate, was "accused" of being a Klansman. Unable, under the law of the Invisible Empire, to admit or deny the charge without a special dispensation "to uncover" from Atlanta, he held off until said dispensation was obtained, and promptly turned the accusation into an asset by loudly proclaiming himself a member of the Klan. He is now campaigning on that issue, and in a speech at Fort Worth declared: "The Klan will continue to grow, and these candidates of whom I speak [anti-Klan] and these great journals [anti-Klan] cannot destroy it." Speaking in a similar vein Sterling P. Strong, another of the five Senatorial candidates, opened his campaign in a speech beginning "I am proud to declare myself a member of the Ku Klux Klan."

It is not likely that the Great American Fraternity will actually enlist as paid members more than one-fifth or one-sixth of the membership of the Ku Klux and the other orders named in the schedule. But with such a nucleus it might well be expected to become a driving force in American politics, for behind it the promoters could reasonably expect to find the sympathy and support of the non-paying, but none the less ardent, haters throughout the land. Consequently, we may expect to read from now on of the increasing importance of religion in politics; of school teachers dismissed for their religious beliefs; of workers losing their jobs for the same reason; of boycotts of merchants for the same reason; and of repetitions north, east, and west of the crimes of ignorance and prejudice which for the past twenty years have been largely confined to the south.

MODERN KU KLUX KLAN [1]

Not from its ritual will the true purposes and methods of the organization be learned. That information is given by its itinerant paid speakers, who are now touring the south and west, soliciting membership. The individual assigned to Mississippi for this work is Joseph G. Camp, formerly a lyceum lecturer, now dubbed "Colonel." His speech, wrung dry of its oratory and its indefinite but ardent praise of "100 per cent Americanism," may be accurately summarized in two paragraphs.

First. The Jews, the Catholics, the negroes, the alien-born are organized; they are a menace to American institutions; it is necessary to combat their pernicious influences; the sole weapon to hand is the Ku Klux Klan; therefore, if you are a true American, join the Klan.

[1] From article by Leroy Percy. Atlantic Monthly. 130 : 122-8. July, 1922.

Second. The morals of the country are in a parlous condition; sexual vice, bootlegging, gambling flourish; the Klan loveth righteousness; if you are on the side of the angels, join the Klan.

The first part of the program is effected by moulding public sentiment, by watching wayward politicians, by combating the sinister propaganda of the press, which is under the control of Jews or Catholics or negroes or foreigners. The second part of the program is the real work of the separate local Klans. It is accomplished in this wise: each Klansman is a "detective"; he goes about his community "with eyes and ears open," spying on the morals of his fellow citizens, the objects of his scrutiny being serenely unconscious of it, as only Klansmen know who are members of the Klan; then, at the next meeting of the Klan, the various members report the bits of information they have collected; the assembled body passes on the guilt or innocence of the accused (naturally, in his absence), and takes such course as seems necessary and proper.

That course is not direct action,—an order to leave town, or a coat of tar-and-feathers, or a whipping, or worse,—as the hired press reports; but selected members remonstrate with the delinquent on the evil of his ways, even warn him; then, should he remain forward and unregenerate, they report him and his sins to the officers of the law, volunteering to those officials, usually spineless, the Klan's aid and comfort; and if they then fail to act, the Klan's duty is to see that they are retired from office and their places more worthily filled, preferably by Klansmen.

The Klan speakers seem always to stress that part of their address outlining the regulation of private morals, and that part is very much the same wherever delivered. But the remainder of the address appears to vary widely from one section of the country to the other, to suit the outstanding prejudice or antipathy of the particular audience being exhorted...

It usually denies responsibility for all acts of violence committed by men in the Klan's garb. But whether such denial be true or not, there is no escape from the moral responsibility for the acts so committed; and I have heard of no criminal in the garb of the Klan who has been brought to justice by the Klan, who alone can know whether he is a member of the Klan or not.

The Grand Wizard is profuse in assurances that the Klan will assist officers of the law. When officers of the law in any community become so helpless and impotent that they have to be backed up by sheeted Klansmen at night, that community is in a bad way. The garb of the Klan does not lend itself to uphold the law; it never was devised for that purpose. The men who first devised it devised it to conceal their identity when doing the lawless deeds that they felt justified in doing. Men who are aiding officers of the law in doing a right thing do not disguise themselves and go about after nightfall. This organization tries a man on hearsay evidence, without giving him an opportunity of being confronted by his accusers, and without lawful authority proceeds to enforce its judgments. The foundation-stone of government and constitutional liberty in our land is the right of a man to be confronted by his accusers and to hear the evidence brought against him...

What is the lure that draws men to membership in such an organization? Why do they fall such easy victims to the cheap oratory of hired itinerant speakers? Partly because of the "jining" proclivities of the American people. Partly because of the desire of exercising power in secrecy and without responsibility. They wish to "get even" with some man or class of men. But in this section and in others the chief appeal has been to religious intolerance. Good men, Christian men, pastors of churches, have enrolled themselves as members, feeling that in some way through this mysterious order they would be able to combat the forces of evil, and especially the political activities of the Roman Catholic church, portrayed in such lurid colors by these new evangelists. There has been a recrudescence of that puritanical meddlesomeness which seeks to regulate the habits, lives, and consciences of other people. The secret methods of the Inquisition all but destroyed the Church of Rome, and for hundreds of years, Protestants, whatever might be their denomination, have gloried in freedom of discussion and publicity; prayer and Christian suasion have been recognized as the means of reaching the erring sinner; yet, today, Christian ministers are found endorsing the idea that men can be made more righteous by a tar treatment applied at night by masked inquisitors.

Assuredly no word of the Man of Galilee can be quoted in extenuation of the unutterable cruelty and cowardice of such treatment. The incident in the Bible which more nearly parallels midnight operations of the Klan than any other is the one in which they came at night to take Jesus, and He said: "Are ye come out, as against a thief, with swords and with staves to take me? I was daily with you in the Temple, teaching, and ye took me not." Since when, among Christian peoples, taking men at night has not been in good repute. They have been told by their chief instructors—Wizards, Kleagles, Genii—that the Knights of Columbus, as a representative of the Great Catholic hierarchy, is on the eve of catholicizing America and destroying our educational institutions; and instead of fighting this hobgoblin, created by their leaders for profit, in the open, according to the manner of their forefathers, they seek to overcome the powers of evil by donning a clown's garb, swearing to conceal their identity, and marching behind an Imperial Wizard, whom they are sworn to obey. They fail to realize that our government has been established by free American people, who will handle it without interference by, or dictation from, church or clan; that it is to be governed by neither priest nor wizard, knights nor klansmen.

The most malign effect of the organization is the destruction of the spirit of helpfulness, cooperation, and love in the community where it intrudes itself. In a community composed of Jews and Gentiles, Catholics and Protestants, white and black, where the life and progress of the community has been marked by helpfulness and cooperation, friendship and harmony, this organization comes to plant discord, racial hatred, religious dissension, and intolerance. Whatever may be its aspirations, it can breed only suspicion and distrust among the members of a community. It paralyzes all spirit of cooperation. It is violative of every principle of Christianity, repugnant to every sense of right, justice, and fair dealing between man and man. Good citizenship should actively and openly oppose its entry into any community.

A NIGHTGOWN TYRANNY [1]

The real Ku Klux Klan worked for a psychological effect, not a physical effect. A white-robed horseman would ride up to a darky's cabin, hand the bridle of his horse to a negro with one hand, reach up with his other hand and remove his own "head," offering it to a negro to hold, saying, "That old head hasn't worked right since I was killed at Antietam." Or a costumed Klansman would come to a negro's shanty in the night and ask for a pail of water. The ghost would "drink" this water in a few gulps, pouring the water into a rubber bag, hidden in his robe. He would then remark, "That's the best drink I've had since I was killed at the battle of Shiloh."

Thousands and scores of thousands of such alarming but harmless incidents were brought about by the intel-

[1] From article by William G. Shepherd. Leslie's Illustrated Weekly. 135 : 329-31. September 10, 1921.

ligent Klansman of the south. The superstition about the Klansmen was spread through the negro world, and historians of both the north and south do not hesitate to say that the Klansmen did much to make easier the transition from slavery to a sounder economic condition.

But—and here is the point on which the movement of today hinges—the leaders among the Ku Klux Klan of those days found that the movement was getting out of their control. They officially disorganized in 1869 the Klan which had been first organized in Pulaski, Tenn., in 1867. Loyal members of the Klan tore up their white robes, destroyed their records and formally disbanded the organization.

Yet white-robed night riders continued to ride. They made full use of all the paraphernalia of the Klan. But physical rather than psychological punishment was their aim, and only too often their object was not to perform punishment but to commit outright crime. The real Klansmen had sought only to subjugate, by superstition, the restless and unruly myriads of negroes who had been set free by Lincoln's proclamation. The pseudo-Klansmen, who came after them, often terrified entire communities, including whites themselves. Life became insecure in many southern communities, as a result of the activities of the alleged Klansmen, and the Congress of the United States was finally called upon to investigate the situation. Members of the original Klan appeared before Congressional committees and testified that the purposes of the Klan had been legitimate. They were "the protection of the weak; the relief of the injured and oppressed; the extension of aid to orphans and widows of Confederate soldiers, and assistance to the government in the execution of all constitutional law."

The objects of this twentieth-century Ku Klux Klan, as stated in an application blank which I secured during investigation in southern states, are far different from those of the original Klan. The creed of the old organization, for instance, provided that members should recognize the "Divine Being." The application blank of today's order has drawn a creed, as well as a color line; the applicant, it has been specified, must be a "white, male, Gentile," a "believer in the tenets of the Christian religion." While the old order, in other words, admitted all white men, the new order has admitted only American-born, white male Occidentals. . .

The aims and objects of the new order resound with fine declarations of Americanism. These, if carried out in legal fashion, would undoubtedly make the United States a better place in which to live. But it is the difficulty of forcing the Klansmen to act in legal fashion which gives the new movement a sinister aspect.

The Grand Wizard recently declared:

In the face of these great objects and purposes, to which every American should and does subscribe, it is ridiculous for anyone to imagine that I, as Imperial Wizard, would allow this organization to degenerate into a lawless institution of any kind.

We are increasing, at the present time, at the rate of five thousand members a week. The increase is double north of the Mason-and-Dixon line.

The only punishment which the Imperial Wizard can mete out to an organization which tends to bring about degeneration of the Ku Klux Klan is dismissal or withdrawal of the charter. This dismissal cannot in any way prevent the former members from clothing themselves in white robes, covering their automobiles in white drapery, hiding their automobile license numbers and proceeding to acts of lawlessness as before...

A list of the activities of the men in white robes in the state of Texas for six months brings to light a situation which not even the state of Texas, much less the "Ku Klux Klan" law of the federal government have been able to prevent. If the officers of the law find themselves unable to control such a condition as exists in Texas, how can a private citizen, member of a weird society, having no power except that of striking from a book the name of an offending local chapter of his order expect to do so? The Texas record for half a year runs something like this:

February 5.—B. I. Hobbs, lawyer, Houston, Tex.; hair clipped, ordered to leave town because of large negro practice. February 8.—Lawyer Hobbs ran out of Alvin, Tex. March 13.—A. V. Hopkins, merchant, Houston, Tex., tarred and feathered for annoying girls. March 15.—J. Lafayette Cockrell, Houston, negro dentist, "punished" by white men for alleged association with white women. April 1.—Alexander Johnson, Dallas, negro bellboy; whipped and branded for alleged association with white women. April 10.—August Beck, cattleman, Webster; tied to pole and beaten. April 26.—J. W. McGee, auto salesman; whipped by masked men at Houston for attempted flirting; fined in police court. May 1.—Red Kemp, jitney driver, Goose Creek; whipped, tarred and feathered; supposed bootlegger. May 4.—Town Marshall Samuel King; tarred and feathered; resigned office. May 7.—Dr. J. S. Paul, Beaumont; tarred and feathered for alleged malpractice. May 21.—Justice of the Peace, Joseph J. Devere, Sour Lake; tarred and feathered. May 24.—John Parks, Dallas, flogged; charged with aggravated assault. June 8.—Dr. R. H. Lenert, Brenham; whipped, tarred and feathered; charged with speaking German and with disloyalty during the war. June 14.—Attorney J. W. Boyd taken from office and whipped on charges of annoying girls. June 17.—Negro James Collins, Belton; whipped and branded, after grand jury had failed to indict him on charges of annoying white women. June 18.—E. L. Bloodsworth and Olan Jones, oil field workers; tarred and feathered and driven out of town. June 20.—Henry Schulz, Wharton; alleged German; tarred and feathered. June 27—Ku Klux Klan at Austin, Tex., posted placards warning against violations of the moral law. July 5.—Benjamin Pinto, found in automobile with woman, tarred and feathered; woman taken to her home. July 8.—Harry Adams, gardener, San Antonio; beaten and choked; released when "avengers" found they had the wrong man. July 9.—Citizens of Beeville met and passed resolutions against Ku Klux Klan offering $100 reward for apprehension of Klan. July 9.—Representative Rountree, of Brazos County, proposed anti-Ku Klux Klan legislation in Texas legislature. July 16.—Judge Hamilton, at Austin, announced that no members of Ku Klux Klan could sit on jury in his court. July 16.—Mrs. Beulah Johnson, white woman; taken from hotel porch at Tenaha, stripped, tarred and feathered. July 16.—W. M. Houpengarner, banker; tarred and feathered and beaten, on charges of infidelity. July 18.—E. H. Peters, Chandler; dragged from his room to automobile, robbed of $200 after severe beating, and thrown from the car, gravely injured.

There were ten parades of local Ku Klux Klan organizations in Texas during the first six months of the year. In some cases donations of money were given to worthy causes. The Houston Y.W.C.A. received $600 after their home had burned. The San Antonio Orphans' Home received $100 from the Ku Klux Klan. The Klan at Wharton, Texas, gave a widow $50. A county judge at Cuero was given $60 to present to a tuberculosis sufferer. The Dallas Orphans' Home received $100 from the local Klan.

I have chosen these examples in Texas because the newspapers there have been actively and aggressively opposed to the Ku Klux Klan, and have kept a careful record of the Klan's activities in the state. Analysis of the cases given above will show that, at the beginning of the year, the Klan directed its attention mostly toward correcting questions of color. They finally worked their way toward settling domestic difficulties, and trying to direct private and public morals by means of force. This means that they turned their attentions to whites rather than to negroes. After half a year of activity one branch of the Klan does not find itself able to stop at the punishment of men, but subjects a white American woman to the most disgusting "punishment." And shortly thereafter, when the Texas courts and Texas citizens are opposing the activities of the Klan, we find robbers using the Klan's costumes and methods to remove a man from a hotel and rob him.

Records of the Klan's activities in other states will show the same tendency of white-robed men—whether they be true Klansmen or not—toward criminal interference with individuals or toward actual robbery and murder. Worthy as are the motives of the leaders of this twentieth-century Ku Klux Klan, it begins to appear, after an existence of about two years, that they can no more keep the new Klan to its high ideals than could the fine old southern General Forrest, when he disbanded it then.

Any careful investigator of the new Ku Klux Klan, who works on the scene and analyzes the deeds of the men in the white robes, must come to the conclusion that the new Klan is a dangerous and unmanageable thing and that citizens who attempt to put it down in their own communities are seeking to protect themselves from dangers that are very real.

In many parts of the south, notably Florida, Texas, Oklahoma, North Carolina and Georgia, citizens and officials both are beginning a strong campaign against the Klan. In North Carolina the State Dragon has ordered the state organization disbanded. The society is too dangerous and, in spite of its fine American platform, too un-American in its plans and operations, to be endured.

HOW ELECTIONS ARE CARRIED IN TEXAS [1]

The Ku Klux Klan is probably stronger in Texas than in any other state; it controls the state politically by controlling the machinery of the Democratic Party; it numbers in its membership probably a majority of the officials and certainly a very large majority of the peace-officers. The calm complaisance of the majority of the population who are not members of the Ku Klux Klan can only be explained by their ignorance of the fundamentals of government. The fact that this organization is setting up a separate government which attempts to rise superior to constitutional government seems not to excite them in the least. They hear of someone being dragged away from his dinner table to be beaten or tarred and feathered, and usually they dismiss it with: "Well, maybe he deserved it." It does not seem to occur to them that the same evidence which convicted him in a secret session of the Ku Klux Klan could just as well have been offered before a district judge and a jury in open court. A friend of mine put the case in Texas recently in the

[1] From article Collapse of Constitutional Government, by Chester T. Crowell. Independent. 109: 333-4. December 9, 1922.

following words: "The issue in this state is whether we are going to have courthouse justice or river-bottom justice." In that particular campaign in which my friend made speeches the people of Texas voted by an overwhelming majority for river-bottom justice.

Before the Democratic primary election in Texas last July there were six candidates for the Democratic nomination for United States Senator. Three of them were members of the Ku Klux Klan. Before the primary election took place the Ku Klux Klan held a primary of its own, an elimination contest in which the three Klansmen were voted upon by Klansmen. The other three candidates were not considered at all. The Klansmen, having selected their nominee, went into the Democratic primaries and voted solidly for the man who won in their Klan primary. In this way they ensured the nomination of a Klansman. When these facts filtered out a large body of Democrats decided to bolt the primary, taking the position that the successful candidate was really the Ku Klux Klan nominee and not the Democratic nominee. These bolters joined with the Republicans and put up a fusion candidate. He was defeated by more than one hundred thousand majority. It seemed to make no difference to the vast majority of the voters that they had gone into a primary to vote their single votes when "the deck was already stacked" and one of the candidates had one hundred and twenty thousand oath-bound votes to start with. In Oregon the Klan is in the Republican Party, in the south it is in the Democratic Party, and when it fails in a primary election to nominate a Klansman it never fails to put up an independent ticket if there is any hope of success.

There are, no doubt, many patriotic men in the Klan who believe that through its operations a higher class of candidates can be induced to run for office. In some localities that hope has been realized, but taking the general averages for Texas as an example or for any group of states, there does not seem to be any notable change one way or the other. The outstanding feature of Klan operations in politics is obviously fanatical loyalty to the Klan group which generates violations of the election laws and then excuses them. That was particularly the case in Texas in the last Democratic primary; largely through Klan activities a campaign fund at least four times the legal limit fixed by state statute, and perhaps ten times the limit, was raised and expended in behalf of this candidate. When the fact that he had violated the election laws was proved against him in the thirteenth district court at Corsicana, Texas, the Klan rallied more loyally than ever to his support. The uncontradicted testimony before that court showed the raising and expenditure of four times the legal limit for campaign expenses.

INTOLERANCE IN OREGON [1]

Oregon vies with Texas and Oklahoma as the state in which the Ku Klux nuisance comes nearest being an actual menace. In Oregon as in other states there is a temptation to over-simplification in describing the Ku Klux Klan. It is not merely a childish outburst of anti-Jewish, anti-Catholic and anti-foreign bigotry. If it were nothing but a Freudian escape for suppressed hatreds of this kind it would have disappeared like a bad dream in the sunshine and invigorating atmosphere of this healthy and sane commonwealth. The masks and gibberish, the appeals to instinctive hostility to the unfamiliar, the play on stereotyped racial and religious prejudices, are all there and they are disturbing evidence of the limits to what education can do even for a selected and naturally intelligent people.

Oregon is predominantly white, native, protestant and typically American. Its early settlers came from the

[1] Survey. 49 : 76-7. October 15, 1922.

south as well as from the north. It has no serious race problem and no reason for acute industrial conflict. Its people are lumbermen, farmers, fruitgrowers, and business men. The workers live mainly in their own town homes or on their own farms and ranches. It is a healthy, homogeneous population, with a low death rate and little illiteracy. Portland is a more representative city than San Francisco, Los Angeles, or Seattle. Her roses, her rivers and her heights are unique; but her citizens are of the best blood, if there are any differences, and her political and social institutions are as progressive and as favorable to the development of the best character as those of any other state.

Why, then, should a Ku Klux candidate for governor have come within five hundred votes of carrying the Republican primaries? Why are there likely to be many of its candidates in the legislature? Above all, why are the people required to vote on a measure which will at one stroke abolish all private schools—whether religious or secular—and require all children of school age to attend the public schools, with an ambiguous exception which is supposed to permit private individual tutoring?

The essential fact seems to be that in our contemporaneous American education—both the formal education of the schools and the more pervasive unconscious education of the home, the church, and the social life as a whole—we are cultivating prejudice, planting seeds of intolerance and bigotry. We are not really encouraging either a scientific or a tolerant temper. We assume that children are to become Methodists or Presbyterians, Unitarians or Catholics, Republicans or Democrats, Prohibitionists, Anti-radicals or what not, and we do not really teach them how to reason or how to think about religious, political, economic, and social questions. We have an easy-going faith or assumption that if children learn to read and to count; if they learn certain historical, geographical, and scientific facts, they will somehow know how to act. It is a stupendous delusion.

KU KLUX KLAN

We reap the consequences in the phenomenon of a Ku Klux movement sweeping over the country and finding even high school and college graduates helpless before its sophistries, its lies, its appeals to our worst impulses. If those lies and base appeals stood alone they would, of course, get little response. Why do they not stand alone? They are interwoven with quite different issues. Our courts and prosecuting officials do not always cope successfully with crime, even flagrant and notorious lawbreaking. This being the case, law and order movements, vigilance committees, societies for the suppression of vice, lynch law, are no novelties in American life. The war increased the business of spying and informing beyond any previous experience. Now comes the Ku Klux Klan to nationalize this tendency; to make it relatively safe by mask and mass action. Everyone who knows of an immune bootlegger, a home-breaker, an abortionist, a radical agitator; everyone who believes that there are such offenders unwhipped of justice; and every neurotic or disappointed person who nurses a personal grievance against society, becomes a ready mark for the Ku Klux salesman. What is more plausible than the program of cleaning up the town, running the offenders against common decency out of the community altogether, not merely fining them after an expensive trial, but putting an end once and for all to their practices, and at the same time giving vent to a little pent-up belligerency and unacknowledged love of deviltry in the ones who are thus vindicating law and order?

In Oregon the Ku Klux Klan has not thus taken the law into its own hands except in a few isolated instances. It is less masked, more open in its methods, than in some other states. It is a direct political rather than an underground guerilla movement. It boldly challenges support. It has its headquarters and avowed candidates. Its goal is the same as in other states—nothing less than complete political control of legislature, administration and courts; and it sees a chance of arriving at that goal without the preliminary steps necessary elsewhere. The struggle is on in the local elections, in the legislative contests and in the initiated amendment, misleadingly called compulsory education.

The difficulty is in seeing through the complications. The issue is primarily one of tolerance, of freedom for education.

The state has an undoubted right to supervise private and church schools, to establish standards to which they shall conform, even to examine teachers and see whether they are qualified to give the instruction which the state deems essential. But the state should not establish a monopoly of education. To set up one type of school and to say that there shall be no other even at private expense would be to put education in a strait-jacket. The state has an indisputable right to tax all wealth and all incomes for the support of its free public schools; but it is not sound policy to say that all children must attend these schools regardless of the wishes of parents. The public schools do not need such coercion and would suffer from the absence of the stimulation of free competition. Variation is, of course, possible within a public school system, but what is needed is the utmost possible freedom of experiment and variation and this a monopolized, closed public school system would not secure.

One extraordinary manifestation of the Ku Klux spirit in Oregon is the sudden fire of criticism against the effort of the Roman Catholic church to promote the spiritual welfare of its own students at the state university. It will be recalled that a few years ago a very well and very favorably known priest, Rev. Edwin V. O'Hara, was transferred by his own desire from Portland to the rural county in which the state university is located. The rural social problem is admittedly pressing and serious and the decision of a competent and successful clergyman to move from what may have been a more congenial city pastorate to an experimental undertaking of this kind was greeted on all sides with enthusiastic interest.

Incidentally it has given the opportunity also to establish in Newman Hall a religious center for Catholic students in the state university. This institution is not on the campus but is conveniently near. There is no charge that there has been religious propaganda from it, or any attempt at interference which the most sensitive critic could discover. Father O'Hara has not sought such privileges as the Y.M.C.A. or Y.W.C.A. have long enjoyed without objection. The natural and logical sentiment of those who believe in higher education by the state would seem to be one of satisfaction that the Catholics have accepted the policy; that they realize that they cannot compete with the university by creating a local college or university of their own; that they will therefore cooperate by encouraging their young men and women to attend the state institution and will themselves furnish that counsel and religious atmosphere which they regard as essential, in such a way as not to interfere with the academic activities of its students. Instead of this we hear that there must be some sinister motive, some desire to displace protestant regents or instructors by Catholics, some deep conspiracy reaching back, perhaps, to a subtle Italian brain or a Sinn Fein firebrand.

It is absurd, of course, and it will probably be short-lived. Whether it is or not will disclose the amount of fundamental common sense, sense of humor, political sense, latent in the men and women of Oregon. The menace lies in the encouragement of hatreds which should be displaced by cooperation, bigotry which should give way to understanding, reasoning by shibboleths which should give way to discriminating analysis. The menace does not lie in Rome or in Moscow or in Tokio; in any race, or color, or creed. It lies in our American complexes, our stereotypes, our traditions, our reversions.

Oregon is passing through a spasm, acutely revealing a general national disease, not hopeless but distressing.

KU KLUX AND CRIME [1]

A ghastly crime was committed at Mer Rouge, Louisiana. Of that there is not a shadow of doubt. Two men were killed after more revolting tortures than the Spanish Inquisition or the most degenerate Roman tyrants ever conceived. Or they died under the tortures. We leave it to the medical profession to say how long a man withstands the shock of successive amputations and the slow crushing of bones. Who committed the crime? That has not been proved. Perhaps it will never be proved. But the belief is nearly universal, and is not likely ever to be dispelled, that the local Ku Klux Klan committed the crime and shielded the murderers.

And from this belief it is only a short step to the belief that the whole vast nebulous organization, with its Imperial Wizard and King Kleagles, its mummeries and monkey-shines, its Kloran mouthings and horrendous oaths, is essentially a criminal organization. By their fruits—and what kind of tree bore the gruesome horrors of Mer Rouge? But that is to oversimplify. We Americans are, after all, a moral people. There is nothing that flourishes widely among us which does not spring originally from a moral intention. Hell may be paved with such intentions but that is no reason for denying their inherent quality.

The men who make up the rank and file of the Ku Klux Klan are, most of them, good citizens, according to their lights. They take America, its present and future, with extreme seriousness. They see grave dangers rearing their heads around them. Why should they not? In every age all men who take life seriously see grave dangers rising against the things they hold most dear. Where men differ is in respect to what is to be held dear,

[1] New Republic. 33 : 189-90. January 17, 1923.

what dangerous, and what methods shall be employed to combat evils commonly accepted as such.

The Ku Klux Klan holds that the dearest values in American life are Protestantism; white supremacy, in America and the world; Anglo-Saxon legal institutions; the system of free private enterprise, or since the word no longer carries a reproach, capitalism. These are respectable values. If one is a Protestant, white, Anglo-American, by blood or assimilation, an owner, present or prospective, of property, why should he not cherish them? Here and there you may find an individual who repudiates the principles by which he counts in life and yet retains his intellectual and moral integrity. Such cases are necessarily rare. Most men have to believe in what they are. . .

And the Klan looks like an appropriate means. It represents organization, the key to effectiveness, in the accepted American view. It is secret, and the American, as a man who talks much and boasts freely, naturally exaggerates the potency of secrecy. In consequence he has always been haunted by the fear of conspiracies, conspiracies hatched by the Pope, the Jews, the Reds, Japanese conspiracies to seize the Pacific coast, negro conspiracies to kill and rob and burn. Shall the devil monopolize the good tune of secret conspiracy? We will conspire ourselves, in the Lord's name. . .

In this great, heterogeneous America of ours a nationwide society is formed, bound to secrecy and mutual support by an oath which, in the act of administering it, is declared to be the most solemn conceivable, whose violation is punishable by death. Is it not inevitable that bitter and homicidal suspicion should often be injected into communities where a society bound by such an oath operates? Is it not inevitable that men should be accused of joining the order to betray it—some falsely accused, some on good grounds? Is it not inevitable that private vengeance should often be exacted through such a form of organization, or by outside miscreants availing themselves of the Klan's name and fame? Is it possible that the law will operate, without restraint and without suspicion, to redress the wrongs committed by the Klan or in its name?

To raise these questions is to answer them. For no one who faces the conditions of American life squarely can have any faith in the statement of Klansmen that the character of the membership is a guaranty of moderate and lawful action. Only the best people are admitted to the order? The definition of "best people" may vary widely from Washington to Mer Rouge. "Best people" in some parts of America appear to relish the odor of burning human flesh. A nation-wide society of "best people" may be anything, and do anything, unless all its acts are subject to full publicity which enables the majority of the organization to keep the minority under control.

But why borrow trouble, it may be asked. The Klan as a whole has not yet departed from its original purpose. When it does, there will be time for respectable citizens to get out. Yes, and to leave behind them the worst elements, equipped with the machinery of secret organization that will enable them to commit crimes with impunity. That is the gravest danger that lurks in a secret organization for political or social ends, like the Klan.

There are few Americans who have not shuddered over the crimes of the Mafia and Camorra, those associations of blackmailers, kidnappers, murderers who terrorize the Italian communities in our cities and occasionally present the police with a mysterious crime to occupy them vainly for months and years. What a good Klansman thinks of those societies it is needless to inquire. Yet the Mafia and Camorra appear to have been originally launched with patriotic purposes not less lofty than those of the Klan. They included, and to some extent still include, the best people, just like the Klan. Crimes were committed by them; crimes were committed in their name. They degenerated to criminal organizations and live on, a curse to the Italian people throughout the world.

There is no room for the secret political society in a civilized state. It may seem to work for good, for a time, but there is no permanent gain from good wrought through terrorism. Sooner or later such an engine runs away from its drivers, and where it will end and what it will destroy on the road no one can foretell. It is the plain duty of every American legislature to unmask the Klan and make its acts and personnel public, before it evolves into a thing against which orderly government will strive in vain.

DENOUNCES KLAN IN WARNING TO MASONS [1]

In one of the most important communications on the Ku Klux Klan issue by any Masonic official in this section of the country, Frederick W. Hamilton, 33d degree, of the local Masonic Temple, who is supreme council deputy for Massachusetts, in a notice sent to Scottish Rite Masonic members, gives warning that no Klansman is entitled to membership in the organization and further points out that "no Scottish Rite Freemason can consistently be a Klansman."

The notice sent out by Deputy Hamilton and headed "Ku Klux Klan," reads in part as follows:

It has come to my attention that Scottish Rite Masons are being solicited to join the Ku Klux Klan, on the ground that its announced purposes should commend themselves to Masons. Some of them would; others should not.

Men and organizations are to be judged by their acts, not by their professions.

The Klan calls itself an invisible empire. There is no place for an invisible empire in the United States. Masonry stands four-square for the United States and its constitutional principles and usages.

The mask is the refuge of the coward.

The Klan can disavow the deeds of masked men.

[1] New York Times. January 23, 1923.

The Klan can claim that masked malefactors steal its livery and bring it into unmerited obloquy. Possibly, but the Klan invites it.

The Klan, secretly and behind masks, tries, sentences and executes the sentences. We have courts and the ballot box for the punishment of wrong-doing and the abolition of abuses. Recourse to other means is not only un-American, but subversive of that order which is one of the foundation stones of Masonry.

Any men have the right to associate publicly for the purpose of accomplishing social and political ends by the formation of public opinion and the use of the ballot.

No men have the right to associate privately to accomplish social and political ends by mystery and terror and outside the law.

LETTER ON KU KLUX KLAN [1]

Mayor Curley addressed the following letter upon the 13th instant relative to the Ku Klux Klan outrages:

CITY OF BOSTON,
OFFICE OF THE MAYOR,
January 13 1923.

A. V. DALRYMPLE, ESQ., Attorney-at-Law, 201-14 Wheat Building, Fort Worth, Texas:

MY DEAR MR. DALRYMPLE,—I have your stirring letter of January 4, 1923, which is instinct with the true spirit of America, revealing the courage, resolution and fidelity genuine Americanism connotes, and without which American liberty must go down before that sham patriotism which thrives in darkness and falsehood, which seeks by violence and terrorism to override the law and constitution of the land and supplant the principles of American democracy by the abominations of organized scoundrelism. I can understand thoroughly the flaming indignation of men like you fighting on the forefront of the battle line for their precious political heritage and facing the meanest and most unscrupulous enemies that ever warred, against the civil, religious and political freedom of America.

Your call to us of the north to aid in crushing this monstrous spawn of ignorance, bigotry, greed and deception cannot and will not go unanswered. The time has come for the sane elements of American life to organize themselves into a body that will stand unflinchingly back of the law and its enforcement; that will not only pitilessly destroy this Ku Klux Klan abomination, but will drive out of the political, professional

[1] City Record. (Boston). 15 : 93. January 27, 1923.

and mercantile life of America the leaders and organizers of the Klan, and the men who have given them their aid and sympathy, openly or secretly.

The men who are engaged in this monstrous conspiracy are public enemies, unworthy of tolerance or mercy, lacking even the condonation of their crimes—insanity—we accord to dynamiters and anarchists. Ku Klux Klanism is a crime against Christianity, Americanism and civilization. It is a monstrous hypocrisy; a cold-blooded and deliberate fomentation of hatred and persecution to enable its leaders and preachers to grow rich on the credulity of their gulls, to secure political power and enable them to transform the American republic into a huge camorra, more odious than any other political monstrosity that has affrighted the modern world.

Unless we destroy it it will destroy us; but destroyed it must be as pitilessly as rabid dogs are destroyed.

The commercialism and greed that are at the base of Ku Klux Klanism are already manifesting themselves. Publicity is one of its feeders, since its grotesque and fantastic methods appeal to the weak-minded and credulous and its nocturnal murders, burning and outrages, call to the criminal and degenerate. Its various manifestations are a challenge to civilization and its government and law; and it is time to take up and answer the challenge. . . .

There is talk of the organization of a protestant society to fight it, since it degrades and discredits Protestantism. I believe every political leader in the state should be placed on record. The decent membership of the masonic order should be called upon to repudiate the so-called Scottish rite now openly in alliance with the Klan in the west. Our motto should be, "Those who are not with us are against us;" and we must institute a rigid, persistent, peaceful boycott against every person, corporation and business that does not stand out openly and firmly against the Klan and all it means. Moreover, I believe pressure should be brought upon the banking interests of the north to refuse capital or credit to the cities and communities tolerating this anti-American camorra, since its reign of terror and persecution makes business and trade subject to the threats of outlaws and outlawry, destroying the confidence on which they are based.

Bankers of sanity can be made to understand this and in the last resort it is the savings of the plain, law-abiding citizens which furnish the capital of the banks here and elsewhere; and those people can refuse to permit their money to be used to finance persons and communities that are public enemies and wreckers of society.

Above all things let us refuse resolutely to tolerate weakness, cowardice or betrayal in the places of authority. Let us stand behind law and order until they fail us; and then we can remember the example of the Italian Fascisti. The peace, safety and freedom of the land must be preserved at all hazards, and daylight and decency, courage and loyalty will triumph over the hosts of darkness and degeneracy.

Eternal vigilance is the price of freedom. The men of the north who broke the might of Germany and saved Europe from its menace are not the men to brook the insolence or recruit the ranks of the Ku Klux Klan. They will war if war be best and if they have to fight to make America safe and its law respected and obeyed, there will be little left to this creature of the night to bury. Ku Klux Klanism must be treated as all forms of treason, outrage and lawlessness are treated, with vigor and without mercy.

It is necessary of course to educate the public as to the true character and purpose of this iniquitous organization; and its rather transparent attempt to pose as one thing south and another thing north, must be exposed; and it must be made to stand naked in the sun for what it is, an enemy of law and order, a foe of Christianity and civilization, a wrecker of civil and religious liberty, a violator of the Constitution, an organized system of murder, torture, arson and outrage, a traitor to God and country.

Let us get rid of this puerile twaddle called "100 per cent Americanism," whose devotees are 100 per cent anti-American. Let us announce our whole-hearted hatred of government by church vestries and secret society lodges; and stand inflexibly for the principles of Washington, Jackson and Lincoln.

Let us be led by men, not midnight marauders. Let our totem be the lion not the coyote, the eagle not the turkey buzzard.

Yours very truly,
James M. Curley, *Mayor*.

KU KLUX KLAN [1]

I am enclosing a copy of the Encyclopaedia Britannica account of the Camorra. The Ku Klux Klan is even more dangerous to the integrity of our own organized government because of its very insidiousness. Primarily an ignorantly conceived scheme—anti-Catholic, anti-Jew and anti-negro—it possessed the appeal of the mysterious and of anonymity. Now it seeks to dignify itself by an assumption of exclusive Americanism and as the knight errant of punishment of certain types of evil-doers.

There is no sort of lawlessness that is so subversive of permanent law and order through governmental agen-

[1] By "A. Texan." Survey. 48 : 251. May 13, 1922.

cies as that which declares to the public that government has broken down and that a secret agency must take its place.

As a fomenter of private hatreds; as a feeder of the flames of religious prejudice; as a breeder of suspicion between friends and neighbors; as a creator of dangerous secret political corruption; as a destroyer of community solidarity; as a fomenter of strife and conflict at a time when our national life is at stake, the Ku Klux Klan is a menace so terrible that I cannot conceive how Mr. Devine should even damn it with faint praise.

Our people are torn with dissension—and men are doubting their neighbors. The Klan has sowed dragon's teeth—and monsters are already springing up where they sowed. The social order is at the edge of chaos, and "philanthropic doubts" have had added the apple of discord. If any good citizenship has turned to the Klan for the administration of law to punish offenders, that very citizenship has belied their allegiance to a government of order. They practically say that they have failed to work openly in behalf of honest and fearless administration of the law, but will secretly condone and join with a lawless assumption of what can only be a governmental function. This latter is anarchy. Regardless of the badness of evil-doers, it is anarchy.

The moment a secret order so feels its power that it can mete out punishment to an actual evil-doer, it is right on the edge of settling private grudges and from that to a very tearing down of all public and private safety.

Read of the Camorra, my friends. If you were saturated with the local atmosphere as I have been ever since this evil thing was born in an ignorant imagination you would feel the same sorrowful dread. You can't know what it is to sit with your family in your home down below the dam and know that there is many a sign that the dam may break. Still, in that event you could move the family to higher ground. But with us—where would we go? To Russia, where Ku Klux pogroms were anti-Jewish? To contemplate the inquisition of Spain against the Protestants as an example of what anti-Catholicism might aim at here?

K.K.K.[1]

By flattering the native-born Protestant Gentile white American, by depicting the United States as secretly endangered by Jews, Roman Catholics, negroes and foreign-born American citizens, a fair proportion of simple jungle-minded folk, all over the country, have been induced to take oaths of red-blooded Americanism. The Kleagles, or salesmen, become solemnly "naturalized" in Mr. Simmons's Invisible Empire. They pledge him loyalty of a kind that no president gets even from postmasters, and they go through "a blasphemous and sacriligious mockery of the holy rite of baptism"—all with a view to their going out for recruits on the basis of a 40 per cent commission.

What prepared the United States for this eruption of primitive supersition? Mr. Lusk and Mr. Stevenson and their secret paid spies and secret volunteer agents are in part entitled to the credit. This is plainly an outcropping in final idiocy of the many tyrannical manifestations with which this country has been afflicted since the president yielded completely to illiberalism and gave Burleson and Palmer carte blanche. It is not so many months since the National Security League paved the way for the Ku Klux Klan. In the activities of that and similar organizations, in the intolerances of the American Legion, in the attacks on civil liberty that culminated in such events as the Albany expulsions, the more jungle-minded Americans have naturally been led to believe that 100 per cent Americanism really calls for an "invisible empire" on the lines of imperial wizardry.

[1] New Republic. 28 : 88-9. September 21, 1921.

Feeble-minded it is, rather than evil-minded; but it is impossible for so much feebleness to become organized without becoming a danger to the people outside the Invisible Empire. Among primitive intelligences everywhere, whether in New Jersey or in the Melanesian Islands, secret societies are likely to be alluring. . . In every American community people ought to know the terrorizers. These born terrorizers do not need to be terrorized in turn. But they do need to be insulated by those who have no religious bigotry, no race hatred, no superstition and no fear.

WHY THEY JOIN THE KLAN [1]

For the student of social phenomena there is rich food for reflection in the fact that all the adverse criticism to which the Ku Klux Klan has been subjected has not apparently hampered the growth of the organization even in the slightest degree. Indeed, it seems as though rapidity of growth and bitterness of criticism must have some direct relationship. In part, this is the result of the natural human trait of sympathy for the "under dog," and especially when he is the object of attacks by the press. In part, it is due to a failure by most critics of the hooded order to make due allowance for the forces which have brought it into being.

No matter how much you may, as we do, deplore the fact, the Klan today has no fewer than two and a half million members, and perhaps as many as four million; the national headquarters alone have assets of about $1,000,000; it virtually dominates the politics of Texas, Oklahoma, Arkansas and Indiana; and is very strong in Ohio, Oregon, Maine, Connecticut, New Jersey and a dozen other states. It has sent Earle B. Mayfield to the United States Senate from Texas, and has kept out of the same body Albert J. Beveridge of Indiana. It has

[1] From New Republic. November 21, 1923. p. 321-2.

gone into national politics with all its might, and to stay; it fully intends that there shall be a Klan candidate for President next year, and that he shall win. Under the circumstances, it is perhaps about time that we should lay aside mere abuse long enough to make an attempt to understand this phenomenon, and the factors in American life which have brought it into being.

It is absurd to suppose that the Ku Klux Klan is composed exclusively of the community's dregs, mere hoodlums who welcome the opportunity it affords for participation in sadistic orgies with the whip. In the south this element appears to be at least an active minority in the organization everywhere, and a majority in many localities; but there are also, both in the south and north (and particularly the latter) hundreds of thousands of Klansmen who are solid, respectable citizens, kind and loving husbands and fathers, conscientious members of their churches. The worst crime to be assessed against these individuals is ignorance, and the bigotry which ignorance produces.

It should be noted that the Klan, as it enters any new community, begins with the leading citizens, and works down. After the first novelty has worn off, it is frequently the case that the rougher and more lawless members get control and set the tone. Though only a small fraction of the members, as a rule, actually participate in crimes of violence, it is by this group and its deeds that the organization as a whole is judged.

The members of the order, then, taking them by and large, are not vicious, but misled. Their very zeal for the maintenance of American institutions which they believe are endangered, has caused them to embrace a philosophy absolutely opposed to the democratic principle. Probably the war, which has become so universal a scapegoat, must also be blamed for the mental attitude which makes prospective members of the Klan. The war produced in many millions of Americans a profound disillusionment and destruction of existing beliefs. The principles of security and justice which were supposed to rule the civilized world were suddenly found to be far less substantial than had been supposed. Moreover, persons with a private axe to grind both then and later spread strange stories about those in authority. President Wilson, for example, was alleged to be controlled by the Jews—"look at Brandeis and Baruch;" or by the Catholics—"look at Tumulty." The "Bolshevist menace" has also been exploited for all it is worth by the numerous individuals and societies which have made a living by selling hysteria; and out in the country districts sober and worthy, if none too intelligent, citizens have had no means of discovering how exaggerated these alarmist statements really were. Finally, prohibition has done its part. The law has been evaded so generally and flagrantly that it is small wonder the average citizen, especially in the small towns, has believed the persuasive Ku Klux salesman who has told him that the government at Washington has lost all authority, and that the people must take into their own hands the task of preserving law and order, just as they had to do throughout the entire west in pioneer days.

It may or may not be true that the Ku Klux Klan will fall of its own weight; but even if it does the conditions which made it possible will not disappear and as long as they continue the danger of a recrudescence of Klannishness, perhaps on an even greater scale, will be constantly present. In the long run, the only answer to the Ku Klux Klan is to offer the people convincing proof that some of the supposed evils against which it is directed are non-existent, and that the rest are being attacked through proper and adequate channels. There is only one sovereign remedy for this disease, and it is education—both to raise the general intellectual level of the community, and to puncture the specific superstitions as to the malevolent designs of any one religious or racial group.

There is undoubtedly much truth in the charge that

newspapers are afraid to discuss with any frankness the affairs of the Catholic church. So are educators, public speakers, and most of all, politicians. It is the existence of such taboos that makes it possible for the Klan to work underground and gain widespread adherence for its fantastic stories—such as the report, for instance, that the birth of every male child in a Catholic family is celebrated by burying a gun and ammunition underneath the church, in preparation for The Day when the government is to be overthrown on behalf of the Pope. Similar taboos exist in lesser degree in regard to the position of the Jew and the negro in the community. There is little hope for improvement in the present situation until all of them are broken, and a healthy atmosphere of free discussion is substituted.

Above all, we need historical education as to what American ideals really are, and as to how and why these ideals are violated by the creed of the "little Americans." Until we are willing to make a genuine effort of this sort, we must be prepared to see either a continuance of the Klan itself or at best, a continued fertility of the soil from which it has sprung, with the likelihood that the whole phenomenon may be repeated at almost any time.

The Reference Shelf

VOLUME II. *Contents*

Subscription for volume II. (10 or more issues), $6.00. Single numbers 90c.

No. 1. STATE CENSORSHIP OF MOTION PICTURES (Briefs, references, reprints)

No. 2. PERMANENT COURT OF INTERNATIONAL JUSTICE (Briefs, references, reprints)

No. 3. LEAGUE OF NATIONS (Briefs, references, reprints)

No. 4. FRENCH OCCUPATION OF THE RUHR (Oxford-Bates debate, with briefs, references, reprints)

No. 5. RESTRICTION OF IMMIGRATION (Briefs, refer., repr.)

No. 6. INDEPENDENCE FOR THE PHILIPPINES (Revision of Abridged Handbook)

No. 7. SOLDIERS' BONUS (Briefs, references, reprints)

No. 8. POWER OF CONGRESS TO NULLIFY SUPREME COURT DECISIONS

In Preparation

No. 9. SUPERPOWER (Briefs, references, reprints)

No. 10. RECOGNITION OF SOVIET RUSSIA (Briefs, references, reprints)

Future Issues to be Announced

www.ingramcontent.com/pod-product-compliance
Lightning Source LLC
Chambersburg PA
CBHW031452040426
42444CB00007B/1064